The TWO RONNIES' Sketchbook

The two Ronnies met socially for the first time at the Buxton Club behind the Haymarket Theatre. At this time, Ronnie Corbett had done three series of Crackerjack! with Eammon Andrews. Ronnie remembers that the script budget for this show was eight guineas. Meanwhile David Frost was looking for comedy actors for a forthcoming series, "The Frost Report." The producer, James Gilbert, recommended a certain Ronnie Barker . . . then David Frost himself saw Ronnie Corbett in cabaret at Winstons and asked him to tea at the Ritz. One result of that historic tea was that two actors named Ronnie appeared in The Frost Report which won the Golden Rose of Montreux for the BBC. Petals of that rose adorn the mantlepieces of some of the writers of this book.

Then one fateful day a certain George Brightwell with a mischievous twinkle in his eye suggested, "What about a show, for those two, called The Two Ronnies". The rest, as they often say when the introduction is getting too long and boring, is history.

This book is a selection of some of the sketches and monologues that appeared in the last six series of The Two Ronnies. So pull up your favourite armchair, start where you like, browse at pleasure — we know that you will enjoy this sketchbook and that's an order.

The TWO RONNIES' Sketchbook

Under-edited and Over-written by
Peter Vincent
Designed in a Hurry at
The Nassington Press

A STAR BOOK

published by
the Paperback Division of
W. H. ALLEN & Co. Ltd

A heartfelt tribute

**Thank you to the Ronnies, for all their help, to Terry
Hughes who produced the first five series and to Peter
Whitmore who took over when they came to take Terry
away; to all those who create the process by which an
idea comes to the television screen by making sets,
music, light, costumes, props, faces, moves with a
camera, marks on the script, a million decisions, and tea
and sympathetic noises; to the writers, for searching out
old scripts in unbelievably squalid conditions and to
Cathie Foote who typed the manuscript and who
convinced us for seven years that the BBC coffee she got
for everyone was 38p a cup.**

Edited by Peter Vincent
Designed by Mike Ricketts and Martin Atcherley
Copyright © 1978 Wyndham Publications
Design Copyright © 1978 The Nassington Press

Photographs of the Two Ronnies by John Timbers
Photograph of Raquel Welch from the Kobal Collection
Photographs of Julie Crosthwait by Rod Shone
Thanks to Ronnie Corbett for pictures from his personal collection, to the B.B.C., Central Press Photos Ltd.,
Mary Evans Picture Library and London Features International Ltd.
Picture research by Annie Horton

Linework by Safu-Maria Gilbert, Vana Haggerty, Nick Kavanagh, Karen Murray, Malcolm Smythe

Thanks to Mike Martin, John Hensley and a Happy Birthday to Thomas Bewick

A Star Book
Published in 1978
by the Paperback Division of
W. H. Allen & Co. Ltd.
A Howard and Wyndham Company
44 Hill Street, London W1X 8LB

Typesetting by The Yale Press Ltd.
Separations by Eagle Litho Ltd.
Printed in Great Britain by Hunt Barnard Web Offset Ltd

ISBN 0 352 30312 3

CONTENTS

THE WRITERS.
Sketcherism Spoon **was written by Dick Vosburgh.**
Inflatin, Dr. De'Ath **and** *An Appeal on Behalf of the Indecisive* **were written by Garry Chambers and Peter Vincent —** *Chute First* **by Barry Cryer and David Nobbs —** *Nine O'clock Newt* **and** *Nows at Ton* **by Barry Cryer and Peter Vincent —** *Rook Restaurant, Repeats* **and** *Party Names* **by David Nobbs —** *Tomorrow's Kitchen* **by Ian Davidson and Peter Vincent —** *Slap-Up Party* **and** *Hello* **by Michael Palin and Terry Jones —** *Cliffhanger* **by Peter Robinson and the rest of the sketches and monologues by David Nobbs and Peter Vincent.**

One of the features of "The Two Ronnies" has always been the amazing verbal dexterity of Ronnie Barker. In this first sketch, about the famous Dr. Spooner, written by Dick Vosburgh, Ronnie was required to mix up his words in the manner of the celebrated Warden of New College. The danger was that he might go and get it wrong, or right, rather ... but we needn't have worried. He got it all wrong on the night . . . . .

SKETCHERISM SPOON

Pompous Theme Music.
Caption: Of Men and Words
(Mix to RC at desk)

RC Good evening. The Spoonerism. "Of Men and Words" deals with a man who was born July 22, 1844. The Reverend William Archibald Spooner of New College, Oxford . . . . . the man who committed such inadvertent verbal transpositions as — "Yes indeed, the Lord *is* a shoving leopard" and the immortal Royal toast: "To the queer old Dean!" A new play opening next week deals with the home life of the spoon who invented the mannerism — er — man who invented the Spoonerism! Here is the opening scene of the play.

(Cut to dining room of the 1880's/1890's. Wife is discovered making preparations for breakfast. Enter RB in dog collar)

WIFE Ah, there you are, William. Beautiful day, isn't it?

> **RB** Quite so — the shine is sunning, the chirds are burping — lovers are killing and booing . . . It makes one glide to be a lav!

WIFE It's just as well you're in a good mood. *(She hands him a shirt)* Because look what the laundry did to your best shirt.

> **RB** Good Heavens. They've freed the slaves!

WIFE Frayed the sleeves, dear.

> **RB** I did that, saidn't I?

WIFE They've also torn the collar and smashed all the buttons.

> **RB** *(Looking closer)* Quite so! It never pains but it roars. Buttons, collar and sleeves at one swell foop! Well, I'll fight them nooth and tail! Naith and tool! I'll go down and smith them to smashereens. *(Goes towards the door)* I'm going to tump in a jaxi!

WIFE William — wait! Surely such a scene would be unseemly for a man of your calling?

RB *(Returning to table)* You're quite right, my dear. After all, I *am* a clan of the moth. Better to let sleeping logs die. To hue is ermine. *(He sits)*

WIFE That's better. Do you feel like some breakfast?

RB Indood I dee! A suggestion to warm the hartles of my — cockles of my heart. I rather fancy some hot toatered bust, a rasher of strakey beacon, and some of that cereal that goes pap, snockle and crap.

WIFE Very well, William. And while you're eating it, I shall be packing my trunk.

RB Tracking your punk?

WIFE Yes, William, you see, I'm leaving you.

RB Leaving me after 20 years of bedded wiss? *(Laughs nervously)* This must be some rather jathetic poke. You can't mean suddenly to destroy my entire lay of wife!

WIFE I'm quite serious, William. I'm leaving and I'm not coming back.

RB But my dear, consider the word of the Highly Boble: ''What God hath joined together, let no son put Amanda.'' Er . . . ''Let no pan soot amunder'' . . . Dear me, I'm getting my tang all tungled!

WIFE Exactly. That's why I'm leaving you.

RB What do you mean?

WIFE It's quite simple, William. I can't spoon any more Standerisms! *(She realises what she's said and screams shrilly)*

7

AN APPEAL ON BEHALF OF THE INDECISIVE

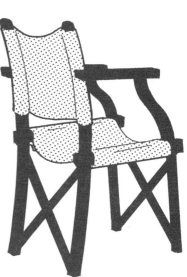

Set: Desk with two chairs behind it. Enter Mr. Nottshawe-Dithering. He is dressed neatly with blazer and four ties, one underneath the other. He has a moustache on one side only. He wears plus fours that are slightly too short. He is about to sit when he notices there are two chairs. He looks at them for a while then looks out into the wings, not knowing what to do. An attendant removes one of the chairs. Our speaker beams and sits down.

Good evening. I'm appealing to you tonight on behalf of the very indecisive. My name, by the way, is Nottshawe-Dithering. Sometimes I'm just Nott or Shawe, but I'm not too sure I like Nott and I'm not sure about Shawe or Shawe-Nott or Nottshawe — or not as the case may be but I'm always Dithering. Now I'm 83 years old. I don't look it but I was born aged 40. I hesitated about coming out, you see. I was then educated at Eton. *(Shows Eton tie)* And Harrow. *(Shows next tie)* And Gordonstoun. *(Show tartan tie)* And this is Miss Wilmott, my governess. *(Show last tie which has nude woman on it)*

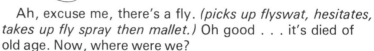

Ah, excuse me, there's a fly. *(picks up flyswat, hesitates, takes up fly spray then mallet.)* Oh good . . . it's died of old age. Now, where were we?

(He leans forward and folds arms then folds them the other way then folds one arm only.) Being indecisive can make life very difficult. When I get up each afternoon, there's this problem of whether to put on my underpants and on whom and which way round or vice versa — but it's worse than that. I'm head over heels in love with Ethel. And Rita. How do I choose? Well, it's six of one and half a dozen of the other — a very exhausting method. Still I'm glad to tell you that this morning I went straight out and got engaged to Rita — *(He points to a framed picture of Rita)* And Ethel. *(He turns frame round to show picture of Ethel.)* And George. *(He takes photo of George out from between other two.)*

Shall I show you a diagram that makes it all clear? Shall I? Why not? On the other hand, why? I know. I'll have a drink while I'm deciding. *(Fills glass from carafe then looks at flowers in vase.)* What lovely flowers! Oh dear I'm going to sneeze! *(Puts down full glass. Elaborately prepares to do huge sneeze, takes out multi-pattern hanky, takes huge breath etc. But he doesn't decide to sneeze.)* How is the Indecisive Society made up and what does it do? Let me show you. Well the society hasn't actually done anything yet but here we are: *(Points to pictogram)*

1% have half a mind to join,

3% are in two minds about leaving,

95% are sitting on the fence,

And Arnold Truscott is simply well equipped —
— with a very tall fence —
— which brings me to my trousers.

I wasn't sure whether to wear plus-fours or not so I wore my plus-two's and kept my options open — which is very cold on the options. *(Sits)* Now where was I? *(Phone rings)* Ah. Oh dear. Mmmm. Now should I answer it? Ah, got it! *(Takes a two penny piece.)* I'll toss for it.

Heads I do, tails I might.
By the way, for really big decisions I use this one.
(Takes one foot diameter penny.)

Now which *coin* shall I use? No problem. I'll toss for it. *(Takes a two foot diameter penny, is trying to toss it when the phone stops ringing.)*

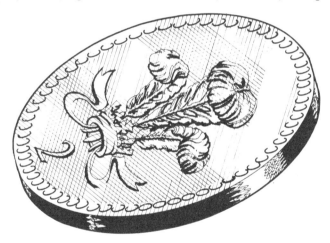

Oh damn!
They've rung off. They always do that.

If *you're* indecisive, do think about joining us won't you? Broken down by sex, and who isn't? — we're 1% male, 1% female and 98% haven't decided. Why not come and help us? Above all send your donations to : The Indecisive Society, 26 Station Road, Droitwich or Uxbridge or Potters Bar, we're not sure yet, VX2 3LK.

Well, I've been invited to drinks with the Chairman of the BBC, so I might go. But I'm not sure if he really likes me so I've got to make a clear cut decision about this. Let's see. *(He takes a dandelion and mouthing 'He loves me, he loves me not', he goes on puffing at it for ever and ever.)*

AD LIBS

Most comic actors can 'ad lib', that is, fill in with lines which are in character, when something goes wrong or someone forgets the words. In the next sketch, 'Dr. De'Ath', written by Garry Chambers, Ronnie Corbett, playing the patient, dropped his medical card and murmured, 'Whoops! Name dropping!' and Ronnie Barker, the doctor, noted, 'Must treat for name dropping' — thus getting two laughs the writer hadn't bargained for. Sometimes a performer will get the bit between his teeth and lengthen a sketch considerably, to the delight of the writer who gets paid by the minute. Long live ad libs! Here's the original — with no optional extras — 'Dr. De'Ath' . . . . .

Dr. De'Ath

A fairly typical doctor's surgery. Identical doors lead severally to the waiting room, a cupboard and the laundry chute. Several filing cabinets, one of them very large and ominous. There is a barometer on the wall and between the doors, a cuckoo clock. Window shows view that tells us we are high up. A large goldfish bowl on side table does not show us the fish. A rubber plant on the doctor's desk is of the trick collapsible kind. As we begin the doctor is asleep with his feet on the desk. A knock at the door is repeated.

DOCTOR What? Oh go to sleep darling . . . There's not a chance . . . Oh! Come in . . .?
(Enter Mr. Billet, a bouncing bright young man.)

BILLET Good morning Doctor *(Glances at card)* De'Ath?

DOCTOR *(Bland and bright as he is throughout)* Death.

BILLET Death.

DOCTOR Yes, nothing to worry about. Very old family. There have been Deaths in Ruislip Gardens from time immemorial.

BILLET Oh, I see. My name's Billet. I'd like to register as a patient.

DOCTOR Really? As a patient? Good heavens!

BILLET Yes well, you're the doctor. I thought I'd better be the patient! Ah ha ha! *(It's his little joke)*

DOCTOR Well now I'll try to fit you in, Mr. Body —

12 **BILLET** 'Billet'.

DOCTOR   Billet! Did I say Corpse? I'm awfully sorry. Slip of the coffin. Now I'll try and fit you in but I'm a popular chap you see. *(Gets a drawer from filing cabinet.)* Here we are — new admissions. *(Blows a quantity of dust off it.)* Oh damn! There's a mouse in it!

BILLET   *(His bounciness returning)* Oh, what's he doing, having a nibble?

DOCTOR   Well if he was he's overdone it. *(Holds the dead mouse up by its tail.)* Ha ha! One moment . . that goes in . . . here . . . *(He puts it in another file. Our minds boggle at what it contains.)* Question is, can I squeeze you in? *(He holds the file drawer upside down. One single medical card falls out.)* Aha! Mr. Grimshawe! You can have his card.

BILLET   But won't he need it?

DOCTOR   *(Brightly)* Not any more.

BILLET   Passed away?

DOCTOR   Dead as a doornail. Funny you know. Fit as a fiddle one moment. Next thing he knew — Pow! Wham! Klunk!

BILLET   What did he die of?

DOCTOR   He went berserk and fell down a laundry chute. We all have to go some time don't we? Though not necessarily down laundry chutes.

BILLET   Well I suppose he went . . *clean* round the bend? Ha ha ha!

DOCTOR   Yes. Well tell me all about yourself, Mr. Billet, while I feed the goldfish . . . I'm an animal lover you know, a healer — it's something in the hands they tell me . . . Where were you born? And what do you enjoy and how often?

BILLET   Well that's going to take rather a long time. I mean I enjoy quite a lot of things . . . *(Trailing off as he watches the doctor lift out the dead goldfish by the tail)* . . and quite often . . . Er, is he asleep? Or fainted? Or having us on is he?

DOCTOR *(Clinking the fish against the bowl)* No he's kicked the bucket. Well there's one fish that's had his chips eh? Ha ha ha! I'll give him to the cat. I know that's what he would have wanted. Tiddles? Tiddles . .? *(Sees cat behind sofa where we can't see it)* Wake up, Tiddles!

BILLET Does er Tiddles always sleep on his back with his legs straight up in the air like that?

DOCTOR Well he has for the last three weeks or so. Oh well. *(Puts goldfish in same file as mouse)* Now you're my patient let me show you round. *(Points to filing cabinet)* That's for medical histories. *(Another)* That's for doctor's certificates — *(Points to enormous cabinet)* and that of course is death certificates.
(During the following sequence we are mostly on Billet's face. The phone goes.)
Hello? Death speaking. Mrs. Dawkins, how are you? *(As he listens he casually waters his rubber plant with a small watering can. Billet watches the plant keel over and die.)*

Oh dear oh dear! What a rotten bit of luck! When's the funeral? *(To Billet)* Have some fudge . . ? No . . .? Of course he was my patient. Tennis elbow. No it's not usually fatal. I'd love to come Mrs. D . . . *(Looks at appointments book.)* But I've got another appointment! Yes it *is* actually . . . Yes, Mr. Willesley. Ingrowing toenail. Yes, there were complications. Well he died — that was one of them. Well Mrs. D . . sorry about your old man . . second husband too. Oh your third? You married again? Well, congratulations! Hello? *(Puts receiver down.)*

BILLET *(Whose face now tells hysteria and panic.)* Yes well goodness, is that the time?

DOCTOR: No, that's the barometer.

14 **BILLET** Then it's high pressure I was going.

DOCTOR No no, plenty of time to bill, Mr. Killet — I mean kill Mr. Billet — *(Takes up card.)* Now are you buried or single?

BILLET Buried. I mean married. Must get home. Wife's expecting.

DOCTOR Wife? Ah! I'm a widower myself.

BILLET Yes, I thought you might be. *(Backs towards door.)*

DOCTOR Poor Millicent! We were so happy. Collapsed in the aisle after the wedding.

BILLET Well they say most accidents happen in church. Goodbye. *(The cuckoo clock cuckoo leaps out and cuckoos once, hanging dead on its spring)*

DOCTOR Don't go. Only one o'clock. Look! The window cleaner's still here! *(We see the window cleaner lose his balance and fall.)* Whoops!

BILLET *(Trying to stay normal.)* See you soon, doctor. Very soon. *(Exits)*

DOCTOR Yes you will. That's the broom cupboard. *(Billet emerges from the cupboard, frightened, filthy, with a large dead bat.)*

BILLET *(Breaking)* And you can have *this* for filing . . . . .

DOCTOR Why? What's wrong with it?

BILLET What's wrong with everything you touch? Well . . . you're not touching me! And I'll see myself out thank you very much Doctor . . because . . . well, look at your flies!

DOCTOR *(Looking at his flies.)* Why

BILLET They're all dead on the floor! Dead!

BILLET And don't bother to come down!

DOCTOR I won't. That's the laundry chute. *(We hear Billet's falling cry . . .)* Oh dear, oh dear . . what a life! Heigho, back to work . . . *(Clicks intercom switch.)* Any more patients, Miss Fosdyke? . . . Miss Fosdyke? . . . . . Miss Fosdyke .

CASTING.

It's a bold writer who ventures to cast one of his sketches and say which Ronnie should play what. If he stipulates a 'very small Scottish man with glasses' they're likely to call in Arthur Mullard and Ronnie Corbett will be playing the bouncer.

So naturally it was Ronnie Barker who played the Scotsman in "The Two Ronnies" salute to the Scottish tourist industry . . .

MACTOURISM

Presenter with aggressively Scottish appearance.

Good evening, Hullo, Scots wha hae and up your haggis. I'm Scottish, by the way. My name is Wee Willie McGorbals *(Caption: Wee Willie McGorbals)* of the clan McGorbals . . . especially after the operation. *(Caption: The McGorbals of McGorbals — especially after the operation)* Now I am President of the Institute of Scottish Tourism. *(Caption: P.I.S.T)* In short, I'm Pist.

Now how do you get there? Well, let's look at the map.

SCOTLAND

John o'Groats
Ben Loyal
Ben Hope
Ben Narna
Ben Hur

Sound of Moosich
Loch Jaw
Loch Anckie
Glen Campbell
Inverness
Loch Ness
ABERDEEN
Balmoral Castle
Marsh of Mallow
Ben Nevis
Pass of Killiecrankie
DUNDEE
Glen Lyon
Ben Lyon
Loch Lomond
Bannockburn
Firth of Forth
Froth of Frith
Fife of Faith
GLASGOW
EDINBURGH
Fjord of Fort Forsythe
Kyle of Bute
The Monster of The Glen
1   40
Flodden Fields
Boat of Angus
Mull of Kintyre
Pyle of Muck n'Mire
W.C. Fields
Castle Douglas
Gretna Green
Kirk Douglas

The Rest of The World

Take the old fashioned scenic route, over the Braes of Altnasporran by way of the Quilt of Skelt, to the Kyles of Bute, where old Angus McFergus will row you across in his old Gaelic skiff if he's not out flashing his sporran and tossing his wee caber down at the Cock-a-Leekie Inn with Inverness Lil and others of that ilk.

Then why not take the road to the Isles? You go up here by Bannockburn . . . *(Begins to get angry)* where in 1314 the patriot Robert the Bruce and his gallant clans routed the trecherous lecherous English rabble who were sent to pillage their native homelands. *(Recovers himself)* You'll be assured of a great welcome at the Bannockburn Inn where you can stand by the fire and sorely burn your bannocks. *(Becoming angry again)* Drive on by the sodden fields of Flodden and Culloden, where the gallant Bonnie Prince Charlie's troops were brutally massacred by the cursed Earl of Cumberland and his gangs of illiterate drunken murderous English thugs. *(Becomes calm again after this outburst)* There's a very nice souvenir shop on the battlefield where you can buy Dr. Hamish Kinley's book of Scottish portraits, known as Dr. Kinley's Facebook. This book is full of people not generally known as Scottish such as the great road makers, Macadam and Maceve. You know the old Scottish story. He said: "Here's an apple, Maceve" and she said: "Ta, Macadam". There's the inventor of radio spaghetti, Macaroni, who also invented McTurtle soup, and the famous Celtic murderer Jock the Ripper; the inventor of dentistry, Phil McAvity, and Ben Doon, the Scottish pouffe. It's true, here are some pictures to prove it. Here's the great Scottish composer Ludwig McBeethoven.

And here's the Mona McLisa.

Now, if you drive round this forty mile long stag, blocking the road here, you'll find nary hoose nor moose nor goose for close on a hundred miles, and why? Because the grasping greedy grouse-shooting English landlords burned out the honest crofters so that half-witted English chinless wonders could massacre the innocent Scottish birds.

Speaking of Scottish birds, visit the birthplace of lovely Flora MacDonald, the flower of the Hebrides and Flora MacDougall, the self raising flower. And if you fancy some highland sports, she's one — or if you fancy a tartan troos, She's one. And what's the price that never varies? That's MacDougall's too.

If you meet with hostility once in a while it's only because you Sassenach footpads have plundered us for ten centuries and now tax our goodly Scottish oil, leaving us mortgaged to the kilt — God rot the English! May they never get tickets to see Scotland in the World Cup when they haven't even reached the last sixteen! *(In his fury he picks up some bagpipes and hurls them angrily aside. We hear breaking of glass followed by bagpipe noises as pipes fall to ground.)*

(Recovering himself again.) So, occasionally, when you ask for a wee dram of whisky, you might get given a glass of Rory MacDonald's Revenge; one part of rancid haggis, one part of distilled ptarmigan, which begins with a p, and so would you if you were being distilled, and one part stagnant bogwater strained in the Trossachs, which is sorely painful.

The danger is that it's exactly the same colour as the good old Glen McSkeekie Malt in this glass. *(Raises glass)* Scots whae hae! *(Drinks, splutters and grimaces.)* — which is even more revolting.

Well that's Scotland for the noo the noo the noo, and that is the end of the noos. Next week my colleage Even Up Evan Up Jenkins . . . of Wales . . . will tell you of the lovely Welsh hills, where you can roam at peace all day without seeing a soul, and why? Because the filthy English invaders plundered and ravished and raped the fair sod of Wales. *(Recovers himself.)* Nice to see you all — and good McNight.

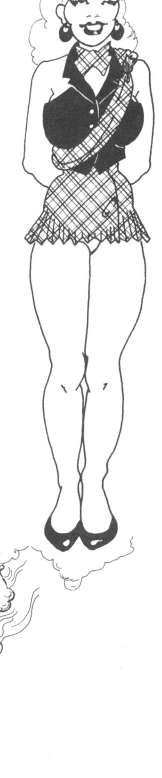

CORPSING!

'Corpsing' happens when an actor can't stop laughing. On television they usually go back and do it again . . in which case the actor is liable to 'corpse' again in the same place. In the next sketch, 'The Complete Rook', Ronnie Corbett always laughed at the moment when Ronnie Barker, as the waiter, sat down at the table. As the audience had to go home to their breakfasts they eventually had to shoot the sketch with Ronnie Corbett hiding behind the menu. Lucky it wasn't Ronnie Barker really . . .

THE COMPLETE ROOK

A restaurant, expensive looking and empty. A well-heeled couple enter.

MAN This looks nice.
(Enter a slovenly waiter.)

WAITER *(Very cockney)* Yerss?

MAN We'd like a meal.

WAITER Oh. *(Digests this information)* For two, is it?

MAN Yes.

WAITER Erm . . . *(Looks round empty restaurant)* I think I can fit you in over here.

MAN Oh, thank you.
(They sit at the table indicated. The waiter pushes their chairs in too far so that they are squashed up against the table.)

WAITER *(Getting pencil from behind ear.)* Yerss?

MAN Well could we see a menu, please?

WAITER *(To himself as he goes for menu.)* They want a bleeding menu now.

MAN Er . . . nice . . . er . . . nice forks.

WOMAN *(Doubtfully)* Yes.

(The waiter brings them a menu. It is shaped like a rook.)

MAN Thank you.

WOMAN Oh, look, the menu's shaped like a rook.

WAITER That's the name of the restaurant, isn't it? The Complete Rook.

MAN Ah, yes. Er, what are you going to have to start with, darling? There's rook paté. Do you recommend that?

WAITER Only when we've got a lot we want to get rid of.

MAN Oh, Well that's honest anyway.

WAITER What about soup of the day?

MAN What kind of soup is it?

WAITER Rook soup.

MAN Oh. Well I expect it's nicer than it sounds.

WAITER It bleeding isn't. It's much worse than it sounds.

MAN Oh.

WAITER Have you ever had forced camel liver marinaded in rain water for five days and pressed through a moss-encrusted balaclava helmet by a pregnant yak?

MAN I think we had that in Morocco.

WOMAN Surely not, darling.

MAN Of course not. I wasn't being serious. We didn't eat stuff like that in Morocco. No, it was Tunis. Why do you ask?

WAITER Because rook soup's worse.

MAN Well why do you recommend it then?

WAITER Cos it's going off. Bleeding freezer's on the blink again.

MAN Oh. Jolly good. Er, shall we choose the main course first and build round that?

WOMAN Good idea.

MAN *(Studying menu)* There's roast rook. Grilled rook. Steamed rook. Braised rook. Ah . . . what's this? La corneille bouilli á la mode de Toulouse.

WAITER Boiled rook.

MAN Oh. This doesn't seem to be the sort of restaurant to come to if you don't like rook.

WAITER It isn't the sort of restaurant to come to if you do like rook.

MAN Oh. Why's that?

WAITER Because we use bloody awful tough old rooks. Full of shot, break your teeth on them, terrible business.

MAN Oh. Still I expect the chef has a magic touch with them.

WAITER Magic touch? Magic touch? Don't make me laugh. *(Confidentially)* Terrible chef. Riff raff. Too much . . . *(Makes Drinking Sign)* Too much . . . *(Elbow Biz)* I'm the only one keeps this place going.

MAN Erm . . . what's this? Queue de cornaille Nantua?

WAITER It's the tails of two rooks in shrimp sauce.

MAN Oh. A sort of pair of rook ends. *(Laughs. Nobody responds.)*

WOMAN You must admit you haven't got a very varied menu.

MAN Nothing to crow over. *(Laughs. Nobody responds.)* I was reading in the Reader's Digest how to lighten awkward situations with humour.

WOMAN Why don't you try it?

WAITER Make your ruddy minds up. I've got other customers to think about.

WOMAN Shall we start at the sweet and work backwards?

MAN Good idea. *(Studies menu)* There's ice cream or ice cream. What kind of ice cream have you got?

WAITER Rook and raspberry ripple.

MAN Ask a silly question. Er, I think I'll plump for rook cocktail, followed by roast rook and rook meringue.

WOMAN So will I.

WAITER Thank you. *(To himself)* About bleeding time too. *(Exits)*

WOMAN We could just walk out.

MAN I don't like to.

WOMAN It's a complete rook.

MAN Well, its name did warn us. We can't sue under the trade descriptions act.
(The waiter re-enters.)

WAITER I'm very sorry. Very sorry indeed. The rook's off.

MAN *(Insincerely)* Oh dear. How awful. Well, we'll be off then.

WAITER We have got a nice roast porcupine with ant-eater dumplings.

MAN Well why didn't you say so? That's more like it. We'll have that twice. Yum yum.

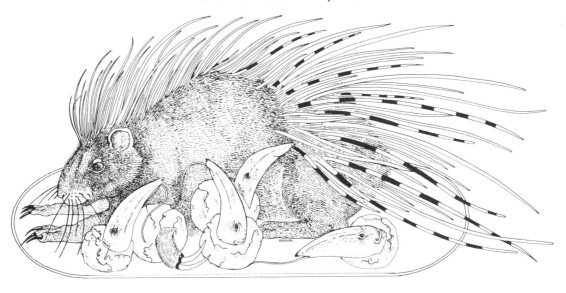

For any reader who's interested in sampling "The Complete
Rook" for himself, here is their current menu —

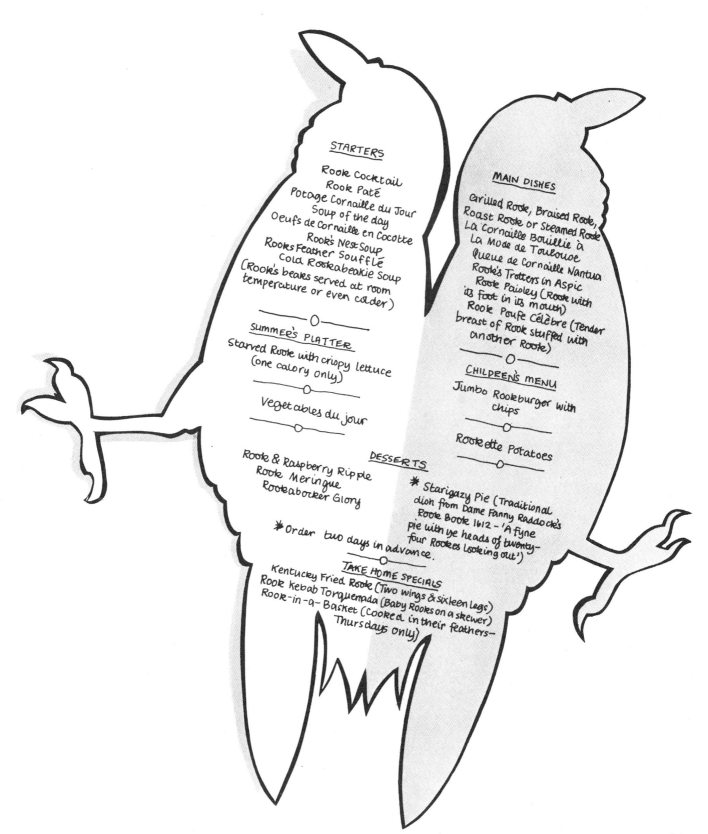

STARTERS

Rook Cocktail
Rook Paté
Potage Cornaille du Jour
Soup of the day
Oeufs de Cornaille en Cocotte
Rook's Nest Soup
Rooks Feather Soufflé
Cold Rookabeakie Soup
(Rook's beaks served at room
temperature or even colder)

— o —

SUMMER'S PLATTER

Starved Rook with crispy lettuce
(one calory only)

— o —

Vegetables du jour

— o —

DESSERTS

Rook & Raspberry Ripple
Rook Meringue
Rookabooker Glory

＊Order two days in advance.

TAKE HOME SPECIALS

Kentucky Fried Rook (Two wings & sixteen legs)
Rook Kebab Torquemada (Baby Rooks on a skewer)
Rook-in-a-Basket (Cooked in their feathers—
Thursdays only)

MAIN DISHES

Grilled Rook, Braised Rook,
Roast Rook or Steamed Rook
La Cornaille Bouillie à
La Mode de Toulouse
Queue de Cornaille Nantua
Rook's Trotters in Aspic
Rook Paisley (Rook with
its foot in its mouth)
Rook Poufe Célèbre (Tender
breast of Rook stuffed with
another Rook)

— o —

CHILDREN'S MENU

Jumbo Rookburger with
chips

— o —

Rookette Potatoes

— o —

＊ Starigazy Pie (Traditional
dish from Dame Fanny Raddock's
Rook Book 1612 – 'A fyne
pie with ye heads of twenty-
four Rookes looking out')

SERIOUS ISSUES.

"The Two Ronnies" has ever been in the forefront when it comes to discussing the serious issues of the day. When the whole vital subject of inflation needed explaining to the nation they were not slow to call in an official spokesman, a large man with a thin moustache . . . . .

INFLATION

THE SPOKESMAN Good evening. I'm the Minister of Inflation. Now, what *is* inflation?

Well, just look what's happened to Twiggy! Ha ha! That was my first joke.

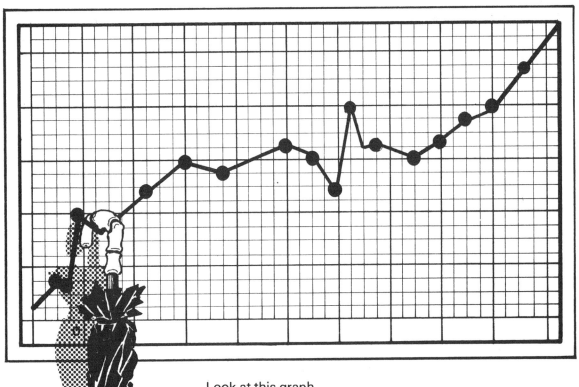

Look at this graph.

It shows the cost of spending a penny at Euston Station every year since 1884. No mean feat in itself. As you can see it's getting very expensive to spend a penny, but the most significant point on the graph is this one. Why? Because I can hang my umbrella on it. *(He does so.)*

What about prices? Trousers for example. *(Holds pair of trousers)* What do we notice? Well, firstly they've got three legs but that's just to be on the safe side. Unless you live in the Kings Road — in which case there is no safe side. Now, trousers are going up alarmingly. What does this give us apart from a pain in the crotch? And what about skirts? Let's look up skirts! They're going up even faster than trousers.

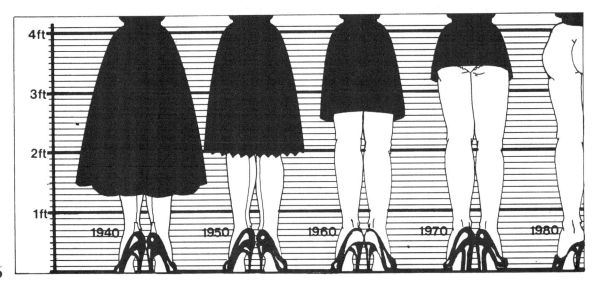

And Y fronts are out of all proportion.

The trouble is, you see, the pound is no longer worth the paper it's printed on. By 1984 paper hankies will be six pounds each so it'll be cheaper to blow your nose on a fiver.

But what about successful and attractive people with sound incomes and a collection of amazing postcards on top of the wardrobe? — I hear someone ask. Well, take me for example. The fact is, my secretary, Miss Rita Crampett and myself have barely got two pennies to rub between us . . . Have *you* tried that? Fun, isn't it? Sorry . . . what I mean is, our gross assets are simply not enough to cover bare essentials, even with accrued interest. And Rita's got extremely bare essentials and some exceptionally gross assets . . . and I've got a very crude interest.

We in the Government are introducing a system known as barter. It does away with your money, something we've been working at for years. For instance this cheque is my fee for a course of French lessons. It says 'Pay Mademoiselle Fifi 10 pounds of rhubarb'. You see? Money's not involved. When they say, 'What about V.A.T.?' I'll say 'Rhubarb'. This yoyo *(Picks it up)*
should buy me a pair of shoes. So one shoe will cost a yo. If a comedian wants a ballet skirt — to each his own — he has to tell a short joke at the rate of two for a ha ha. So a small tutu costs a minihaha. Simple.

How does it all work? Take my wife. She's worth a cow and a sheep. My mother-in-law? Just a cow. They could buy each other and I'd be left with a sheep. Then I could put the sheep on a horse and win a thousand hamsters in the two thousand guinea pigs.

However, I've suggested an even simpler system and the Chancellor of the Exchequer has given his full support — though what it's full of I can't tell you. My plan is to replace money with dogs.

Here's a rough example.

And here's a smooth example.

The system is decimal, ten poms to the poodle, ten poodles in a piddle and a hundred dog pees in the dog pound. Here, for example is a diagram of Rita Crampett's holdings:

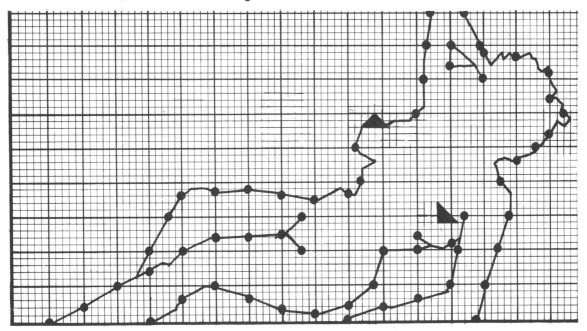

She holds only two pekes. I'll look into that later. But it all works well. Yesterday at Christies a Constable went for a Great Dane and a Great Dane went for a postman, so there you have it. If you send for our government pamphlet on inflation I'll slip in a very nice nude picture of Miss Crampett. Five pounds should cover it. On the other hand she's a big girl. So make it a tenner. Goodnight.

RUMOURS

A party. Arthur Potts is nursing a drink. George Harris approaches.

GEORGE   Hullo . . it's Arthur Potts, isn't it?

ARTHUR   George! George Harris! I've been hearing a lot about you. Still, I don't believe a word of it.

GEORGE   Oh. Good . . . Good . . . What?

ARTHUR   Nothing. Absolutely nothing . . . How *is* the wife-swapping?

GEORGE   What?

ARTHUR   The wife's whopping . . . the wife's whopping great . . .

GEORGE   Come on, her whopping great what?

ARTHUR   Her whopping great . . . uncle . . . her great uncle in Wapping . . how is he?

GEORGE   She hasn't got a great uncle in Wapping.

ARTHUR   Oh . . . Well, it just shows, you mustn't believe everything you hear.

GEORGE   Have you been hearing rumours about me or something?

ARTHUR   Rumours? No. Not a bit. Not a word. Disgusting, I call them.

GEORGE   You have been hearing rumours about me!

ARTHUR   Well, I . . . I . . . I just heard rumours that there *were* rumours.

GEORGE   What rumours?

ARTHUR   Well, . . . you know . . . that you lead . . you know . . . a full social life . . . that you and your wife . . . and other people . . . and their wife . . . you get together . . . and . . . have fun.

GEORGE   *(Hurt)* How could you, Arthur? How could you believe that I . . . you know.

ARTHUR   Oh, I don't believe it. I tell them: 'George, a . . you know? That's a good one. *He's* too moral to swap a stamp'.

GEORGE   Oh. Good. Because I thought it might be rather nice if you and your wife would come over some time.

ARTHUR   Lovely idea. Lovely. Love to. *(Gets out Diary)* Oh, what a shame. *(Opens diary)* We can't tomorrow. We're dining with the . . . *(Hunts through diary)* The Full-Moons. And the next day . . . blast it . . we've got lighting up time. And then we're busy right through till . . . *(Thumbs through diary)* . . . the London Underground map.

GEORGE   *(Drily)* Oh . . well I wouldn't want to spoil your dinner with the Full-Moons.

ARTHUR Look, don't think we don't want to come. God, we want to.

GEORGE *(Drily)* It's just bad luck about lighting up time.

ARTHUR Rotten luck . . .

GEORGE I say isn't that your wife over there? *(Indicates a very attractive woman in small group of men.)*

ARTHUR *(Very hastily and definitely, standing between George and the attractive woman, and jumping up, moving from side to side etc to block George's view.)* No. No. No, it isn't. I don't know who it is. It's somebody else. *(Looks round nervously. His wife, the attractive woman, waves and smiles.)*

WIFE Hullo, darling.

ARTHUR Oh . . that one . .*She's* my wife. I thought you meant . . . *(Sees there are no other women in the group)* the lamp standard. Silly of me. How could it be?

GEORGE I must say she's very attractive.

ARTHUR Isn't she?

GEORGE She's *very* attractive.

ARTHUR *(Pleased)* Isn't she?

GEORGE Very very attractive. My word. Woof!

ARTHUR Isn't she? . . . No, she isn't. She's ugly. Horrible. Repulsive. Frightful old bag . . . warts . . . covered in warts.

GEORGE *(Hurt)* You do! You think I'm going to try and . . . and . . . you know.

ARTHUR No . . I've heard the stories, it did cross my mind, but honestly, I don't. *(Puts friendly arm round George)*

GEORGE Because I was thinking, if you really don't think . . . that . . .

ARTHUR Honestly, I couldn't don't more.

GEORGE That it might be rather fun if the four of us . . .

ARTHUR *(Backing away)* No. Sorry, George. No dice.

GEORGE I wasn't going to suggest dice.

ARTHUR Look, cards on the table.

GEORGE Or cards.

ARTHUR The fact is, Phyllis and I, we may be old-fashioned, but we don't.

GEORGE Oh. I'm sorry to hear that.

ARTHUR Oh, we do *that* . . . *that* . . . but we don't do the other.

GEORGE Oh.

ARTHUR And now I must be off . . . my wife has something in the oven.

GEORGE Congratulations.

ARTHUR Oh, not that oven. The other oven. The electric one.

GEORGE You know for one moment there when you said you didn't . . . *(Laughs)* I thought what they say might be true.

ARTHUR *(Joining good-humouredly in George's laughter)*
Yes. I know. Absolutely . . . What?

GEORGE Nothing. Nothing.

ARTHUR No, come on, what did you mean?

GEORGE Nothing. I never believed it for a moment.

ARTHUR What? Believed what?

GEORGE I mean, I stuck up for you, Arthur. I said to them, I said: 'How can he be? He's married'.

ARTHUR What?

GEORGE Well of course I know some of them are married. But not you. I mean you are married. But you aren't one of them. I mean, I said to them: 'He's got three children'. Of course I know that doesn't prove anything, but . . . well . . . I mean . . . *(Mops brow in embarrassment)* . . . How are the roses?

ARTHUR Surely you don't believe that I'm . . . that . . . any more than I think you're . . . that.

GEORGE No, of course I don't believe it.

ARTHUR Honestly?

GEORGE Never entered my head.

ARTHUR Because . . . meeting you again . . . it would be nice to be friends again . . . We had some good times, didn't we, George? *(Puts friendly arm round George.)*

GEORGE Wonderful times! Just take your arm away, please.

ARTHUR Now look here . . . oh, come off it, George . . . you know I'm not a . . . you know . . . you know I'm not . . . just as I know you don't . . . you know . . . I mean it's all a load of old . . you know.

GEORGE Yes. Sorry . . . you can put your arm round me, if you like.

ARTHUR No, it's all right . . . Thanks all the same . . . Silly believing all these rumours.

GEORGE Nothing in them.

ARTHUR Cheers.

GEORGE Cheers.

ARTHUR *(Very directly)* If you *are* doing any wife-swapping, can we join in?

GEORGE *(Very directly)* Well of course you can, you old pouf.

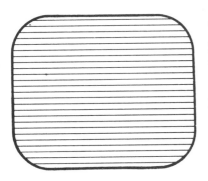

The joy of writing for the two Ronnies is that you know you'll always get the best possible performance of the words. Unfortunately, the script alone of Barry Cryer's 'Nine O'clock Newt' cannot quite do justice to the inspiring sight of Ronnie Barker's hopelessly drunk politician as he meanders in to make a party political broadcast — with a rose behind his ear. But try and imagine it . . . . .

NINE O'CLOCK NEWT

Set up for party political broadcast. But chair is empty.

VOICE OVER There now follows a Party Political Broadcast . . . There now follows a Party Political Broadcast.

M.P. in dinner jacket enters with great steadiness. His bow tie is verging on the vertical. He has a rose behind one ear and a dab of lipstick on one cheek. He stands by the chair wondering what to do.

M.P. Good evening. *(He notices chair. He lowers himself into the chair.)* Good evening. *(He tries to lean his elbows on the table but finds it too far away. He pulls the table back to the chair.)* Good evening.

I am not the person you expected to see here tonight. Oh no. Actually, he . . . Sir Hector . . . Thing . . . has been unalaidably devoid — in Amsterdam . . terdam . . . terdam. And I have stepped into his breach as it were at very short indeed.

I've just come from a hell of a party . . a hell of a party conference, where we thrashed out several important

 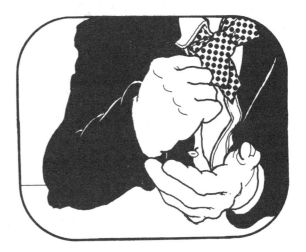

people, including no less a man than the shadow . . . *(Sings)* of your smile . .terdam . . . terdam . . . *(He gets lost).*

Good evening. And I hope you are having one, and if you are having one, tally ho! *(A hand slides in and puts a note in front of him. He focuses on the note.)*

What Britain needs at this moment in our history is *(reads:)* 'Scotch Broth 16p'. *(He turns the note over)* But there are two sides to this. I've just been handed several letters which says, and I quote, 'Pull yourself together. There's a nose behind your ear.' *(He waves his finger as if making a telling point.)* 'A *nose* behind your ear . . .' I think, in a sense, there's a nose behind everybody's ear. And I'm not talking through the back of my neck when I say this. Isn't that the recipe for the ideal politician? A nose behind his ear? He can sniff the wind, listen to his nose, and of course smell his ear. Precisely. What? Some people say, oh yes, it's easy for him to sit up there . . . *(His elbow slips off the table)* But you know, it isn't.

(On a table near him are several objects which have gone up in price. They have labels on them reading e.g. 1967 — £1. 1972 — £3! Looking rather vaguely round he lights on these objects.) Ah! Prices! This used to cost a mere 1967, and now in this year of grace £1 — 40p — just look at it! This railways tickets . . . *(Holds up large representation of a railway ticket)* . . No wonder fares have doubled. You have to buy another seat to put the ticket on! *(Takes out hanky and mops the nose behind his ear.)*

Next. Social hic-wality. I beg you pardon. Equality. Hic! Our position is and always has been . . . *(Takes a lady's shoe out of his pocket)* There's a shoe in my pocket . . . And why not? What this country needs — and I'm speaking off the cuff — is *(Looks at cuff)* 'Strict discipline. Rita. Evenings after six.' She'd put Britain back on its feet. Europe! The G.C.E.! Are we to go round and round and round *(His chair swings all the way round)* — Europe, tail in hand, cap between our legs? And what about Brussels? They're 18p now. Ah! *(Picks up phone)* Room service? I asked for two black coffees and the Daily Telegraph. *(Remembers where he is.)* Oh. In conclusion I'd like to leave you with this thought. *(He falls asleep.)*

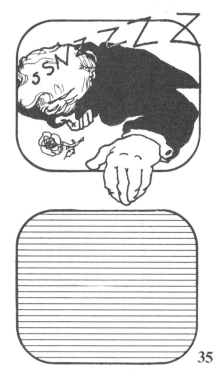

JULIE CROSTHWAIT.
In the Sketch 'Jealousy', the two Ronnies played
opposite Julie Crosthwait.

It behoves us to remember that of a Sunday, while you
and I are pottering on the allotment or flicking a casual
duster over the car, the Rons are slogging away in a hot
studio with such as Julie . . . . .

JEALOUSY

A pub. James and the very beautiful Antonia are standing at the bar, drinking. Enter the smaller Roger.

JAMES Hullo, Roger. Long time no see.

ROGER Hullo, James.

JAMES I don't think you've met the little woman have you? Roger — Antonia.

ROGER How do you do? *(Holds out his hand.)*

ANTONIA How do you do?

JAMES Keep your hands to yourself. *(Knocks Roger down just before he can shake hands. Then he bends over him, horrified.)* I'm sorry. I am sorry. I don't know what came over me.

ROGER *(Getting up)* I . . I . . was only going to shake hands.

JAMES Of course you were. Sorry. Look, what are you drinking?

ROGER Whisky, please.

JAMES Large whisky please. Look, take no notice of me. Go on. Shake hands.

ROGER Oh. Yes. Right. Thank you. Hullo. *(Shakes hands with Antonia. With a cry of rage James knocks him down.)*

JAMES Oh I am sorry! I . . . let me help you up. *(Helps Roger up.)*

ROGER Look, I was only trying to be polite . . .

JAMES I *know!* I get so jealous, that's all. So infernally jealous! *(Hands Roger his drink.)* Bygones be bygones eh? Cheers.

ROGER Cheers.

ANTONIA Cheers. *(They drink.)*

JAMES You two — *haven't* met before have you?

ROGER No. I've never had the pleasure.

JAMES Pleasure?? What? I should hope not indeed! How dare you even suggest it! *(He pins Roger back against the bar.)*

ROGER I . . . I only meant . . . I hadn't had the pleasure of meeting your dear good . . .

JAMES *(Cutting in on the word 'your')* Sorry! Sorry! *(Lets go of Roger)*

ROGER . . . but I've heard a lot about her.

JAMES What?? *(Pinning him up against the bar again)* What have you heard? Come on — What's the gossip, eh?

ROGER Nothing, I heard . . I heard that she's happy with you. Also that you're happy with her. And they even say you're very happy together . . .

JAMES *(Letting go)* I'm sorry. I really am sorry.

ANTONIA You've no idea how jealous he is. He won't let another man so much as look at me.

ROGER *(Turning to her)* Really? *(Turning away again as he suddenly realises that he's looking at her.)* Er . . . What an interesting fire extinguisher!

JAMES I've really behaved badly. It's inexcusable. Look, have another drink. Same again barman . . I really am sorry.

ROGER It's all right.

JAMES Still, you'd be jealous if your wife was as gorgeous as Antonia, wouldn't you? Not that yours isn't. She is. *(Hands Roger his drink)* Cheers!

ROGER Cheers.

JAMES But Antonia is awfully lovely isn't she?

ROGER Yes — gorgeous!

JAMES You cad! *(He knocks Roger down.)* . . . I'm awfully sorry. I didn't hurt you did I?

ROGER *(Getting up and checking for injuries.)* Er not all that much. No . . . *(Winces)* I can still feel most of my parts . . .

JAMES Oh good! It's just that I can't bear anyone to admire her. Yet how can I expect them *not* to?? I mean, she's *gorgeous* isn't she?

ROGER She's lovely . . . No she's not! She's horrible. Ugly. I've seen tattoo'd East German turnip manglers who're prettier than her. *(Antonia knocks him down.)*

ANTONIA I'm sorry! Oh Roger, I'm so sorry! I know you didn't mean it.

ROGER *(Staggering slowly to his feet.)* I . . was only saying that so I wouldn't get knocked down. You're really very lovely!

JAMES Graaaa! *(Smashes Roger down. Roger very slowly begins to get up.)*

ROGER You're . . . average . . . You're the only person I've ever met who's as average as you are.

JAMES O dear oh dear! Look, I'm so sorry about all this.

Good heavens we're adult people! Both of us hitting you like this . . . what will you think? Let's bury the hatchet eh? Look, you two kiss and make up eh?

ROGER Er . . well . . yes . . I'd love to . . in theory. But do you promise me on your honour — on your *Scout's* honour — not to hit me at all?

JAMES Of course I do! Scout's honour. *(Salutes)* Up the Woodpeckers!

ROGER Oh, thank you. *(Kisses Antonia. James belts him one. for a moment he's really down and out.)*

JAMES Oh, I'm sorry!! I never told you — I was thrown out of the Scouts . . . Will you ever forgive me? I couldn't *bear* it if our long standing rapport was broken.

ROGER . . . I think mine *might* be broken . . . *(Begins to drag himself up.)*

(Enter Rupert, a very large man indeed.)

RUPERT *(Heartily)* Hullo James! How are you? Hullo Antonia — you look good enough to eat! *(Embraces her. James looks perfectly complacent about it although Roger is looking at him waiting for his reaction.)* Well, must be off — chin chin James!

JAMES *(Calmly)* Cheers.

RUPERT Come on Sexy. *(Slaps her on the bottom. They go off.)*

ROGER *(Furiously)* Oh! so you don't hit *him* do you?? He's too big. No jealousy *now.* You let *him* take her away from you!

JAMES Why shouldn't he? He *is* her husband.

(Collapse of small party.)

DOCTORS
ANONYMOUS

DOCTORS.

Did you know that the number of people who claim to have seen U.F.O.s is now greater than the number who claim to have seen their doctors? Close encounters of a medical kind are getting so rare that chronic mediphobia (a morbid excitement at the prospect of seeing one's doctor) is now a recognized disease for which the doctors have as yet no cure.

We thought it high time to hear the point of view of the doctors so we asked a senior member of the profession to speak anonymously. Unfortunately he was able to come . . . . .

Good evening. I'm a doctor. *(Caption: A doctor)* Thank you. Now I'm not allowed to reveal my name for reasons of professional etiquette. I fully agree with this and so does my wife, *Mrs.* Poncett-Wilberforce. And of course I'm not allowed to reveal my address but here is an eye test card:

523
A Harley
Street W1

But, I hear you ask, because I don't have a national health hearing aid — what's wrong with the doctors? Well, the answer is: nothing. It's the patients. For a start, you're ill. A recent survey showed that $99\frac{1}{2}$% of patients had something wrong with them — and the other half was a malingering dwarf.

So where do you come in? Well, I'm hoping that you won't. If you wake up every morning feeling something terrible, get a divorce. Ha ha! A joke. No, seriously, if you catch something, it may be catching so don't send for me. I might not have had it. Especially if it's before breakfast. Ha ha! Another joke. And don't come and *see* me either. The last place you should be if you're ill is my draughty unheated surgery. And people come to me with such trivial complaints! A man came to me this morning and said, 'Doctor, there's something hopping about inside my head.' I sent him away with a flea in his ear. Only yesterday I dealt with one case of gross obesity, two cauliflower ears and no less than three broken legs. Here's a picture of him.

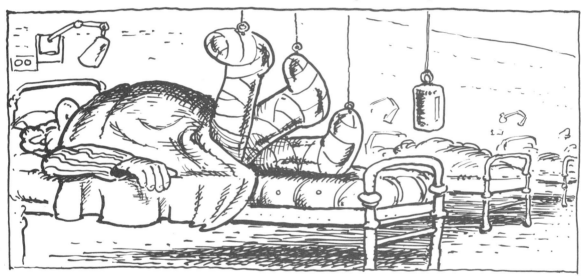

Now, if you *must* come to and you get past my receptionist and the dog patrols, we've got to go through the whole dreary business of diagnosis. Now, diagnosis is like diarrhoea only you get it in your gnosis instead of your rhoea. I suggest that before you come and waste my time you take certain steps, namely diagnose your trouble, suggest some treatment, take some medicine and get yourself well again.

Now, how do you do this? For a start you should examine yourself with this stethoscope. If what you're looking at is very small then use a microscope, and bad luck! *(Takes stethoscope.)* You'll notice it's got three ends.

You put one end in your right ear, one under your left armpit and this bit in your mouth. This way you can talk to yourself, listen to your armpit and play 'Amazing Grace' all at the same time.

Which reminds me, here is a medical profile of my nurse, Amazing Grace.

Isn't she amazing?
   To help you further, here is something absolutely revolting in a pickle jar. To a trained doctor there's no doubt about what that is, either a ruptured spleen or else a rather dodgy jellied eel.

45

The second step in diagnosis is to take your pulse. Now here's a graph of my pulse rate this morning. As you see, a steady 65. Then Grace came in. A steady 100. Here, she took off her coat — up to 165. Here she happened to spill something on her overall and had to take it off. 350 and rising. At this point she happened to spill something on all her underclothes . . . you'll see there's no recording here. Well, would you stand about taking your pulse at a time like that? Then her mother came in. You'll see my pulse rate drops to three. Here, her mother took off her coat — and you'll see that I'm clinically dead.

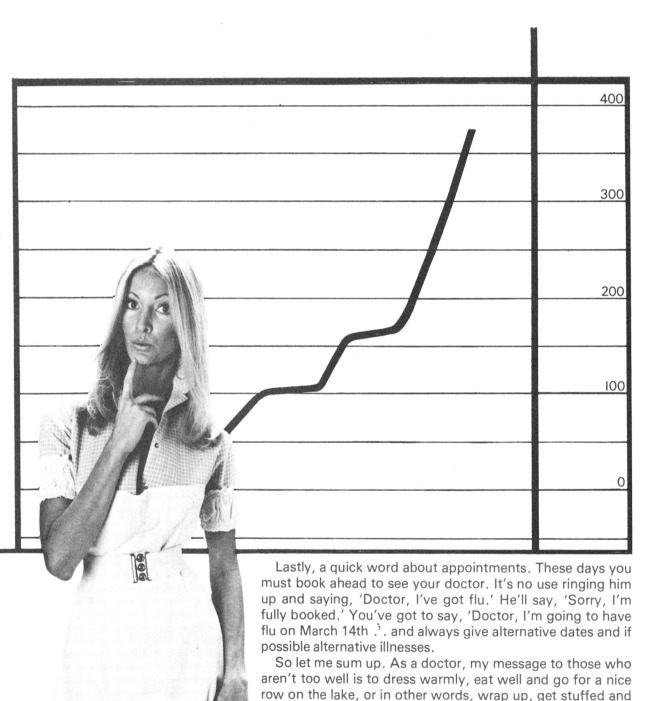

400

300

200

100

0

Lastly, a quick word about appointments. These days you must book ahead to see your doctor. It's no use ringing him up and saying, 'Doctor, I've got flu.' He'll say, 'Sorry, I'm fully booked.' You've got to say, 'Doctor, I'm going to have flu on March 14th .'. and always give alternative dates and if possible alternative illnesses.

So let me sum up. As a doctor, my message to those who aren't too well is to dress warmly, eat well and go for a nice row on the lake, or in other words, wrap up, get stuffed and shove off. Good night.

REPEATS
REPEATS
REPEATS
REPEATS
REPEATS
RE

A party scene. Wilkins approaches Prothero.

> **PROTHERO** Hello.

WILKINS Hello.

> **PROTHERO** Nice day.

WILKINS Nice day.

> **PROTHERO** Warmer than yesterday.

WILKINS Warmer than yesterday.

> **PROTHERO** Look, would you mind not repeating everything I say?

WILKINS Sorry, Awfully sorry. My name's Arthur Wilkins by the way.

> **PROTHERO** Hello. I'm George Prothero.

WILKINS Hello. I'm George Prothero.

> **PROTHERO** You said you were Arthur Wilkins.

WILKINS You said you were Arthur Wilkins.

> **PROTHERO** Oh my god, you're doing it again.

WILKINS Oh my god, you're doing it again.

> **PROTHERO** Look, would you remind not repeating everything I say? There are more repeats with you than with the BBC!

WILKINS Sorry. Awfully sorry. *(Pause)* I bought a colander in Tamworth yesterday.

> **PROTHERO** That's better.

WILKINS That's better.

> **PROTHERO** Oh no.

WILKINS Oh no.

> **PROTHERO** Stop it.

WILKINS Stop it.

> **PROTHERO** Look, I may be unusual but I find it very irritating when you keep repeating what I say. It's not what I regard as the art of conversation.

WILKINS Sorry. Awfully sorry. I have this nervous compulsion, you see. I repeat what people say three times, and then I don't repeat them once, and then I repeat them three times again, and then I don't repeat them once again, and then I repeat them three times again, and then I don't repeat them again.

> **PROTHERO** My God, that's awful.

WILKINS My God, that's awful.

PROTHERO   The thing to do is to get through my next two remarks quickly. Knickers.

WILKINS   The thing to do is to get through my next two remarks quickly. Knickers.

PROTHERO   More knickers.

WILKINS   More knickers.

PROTHERO   Good. Now perhaps we can get some sense. How long has this dreadful complaint been going on?

WILKINS   Good. Now perhaps we can get some sense. How long has this dreadful complaint been going on?

PROTHERO   You've just repeated me a fourth time.

WILKINS   Yes. I think it must be getting worse.

PROTHERO   I believe you're a fraud.

WILKINS   I believe you're a fraud.

PROTHERO   I'll fox you. To escort an orang-outang from Baden-Baden to Wagga Wagga via Addis Ababa or vice versa is enough to make a Ghurka Sherpa commit hara-kiri.

WILKINS   I'll fox you. To escort an orang-outang from Baden-Baden to Wagga Wagga via Addis Ababa or vice versa is enough to make a Ghurka Sherpa commit hara-kiri.

PROTHERO   Rumanian dalmatians hate Tasmanian alsatians and Tasmanian dalmatians hate Rumanian alsatians. Tasmanian alsatians hate Rumanian dalmatians but Rumanian alsatians like Tasmanian dalmatians. Tasmanian alsatians hate Rumanian alsatians. So Tasmanian alsatians hate Rumanian alsatians and dalmatians but Rumanian alsatians don't hate Tasmanian dalmatians or alsatians.

WILKINS   *(After a pause)* Sometimes I only repeat things twice.

PROTHERO   You're a fake. I'm not talking to you.

WILKINS   You're a fake. I'm not talking to you.

PROTHERO   *(To party at large)* That man's a fake

ALL   That man's a fake.

PROTHERO   Oh no.

ALL   Oh no.

The last sketch, 'Repeats', written by David Nobbs, who also created Reggie Perrin, and who didn't get where he is today without taking the Northern line to High Barnet, perfectly utilised the Ronnies' strong points, Ronnie Barker's silver tongue and Ronnie Corbett's perfectly timed reactions. The line, 'Sometimes I only repeat things twice' had to have before it a pause of precisely the right length — and on the recording day, there it was.

Sometimes a sketch depends solely on word play, in which case it mustn't hang about. It's got to rattle on and get off quickly. The next monologue, 'Nows at Ton' starts with a very unlikely contrivance and continues with a single joke repeated in various different ways. But Ronnie Barker's puzzled, lumbering newsreader seemed to make it more than just word play.

NOWS AT TON

NEWSREADER Good evening. Here is the News. *(The phone on his desk rings. He picks it up.)* Yes . . . Yes . . . Right. I see. Thank you. *(He puts the phone down.)*

I'm sorry about that. It appears we've had a slight problem with the News. Our new electronic typewriter has developed a minor fault and it's been typing ''O''s instead of ''E''s. I hope you'll bear with us . . . . *(He picks up papers and starts to read.)*

Good ovoning. Horo is tho Nows at Ton.

At Choquors today, tho throo party loaders hold a mooting to discuss a coalition and this country's oxcoptionally sorious oconomic scono.

Tho conforonco was followod by an apportizing moal of roast boof and bootroot with jolly and croam. Aftorwards dologatos hoard a spooch by ox-Foroign Socrotary, Sir Aloc Douglas Homo. In a short addross Mistor Onoch Powoll said Sir Aloc had his koon support.

Hor Majosty the Quoon was at Homol Hompstoad today to unvoil a momorial to sovoral groat Onglish mon of lottors and poots, including Anthony Trollopo, H.G. Wolls and Hilairo Bolloc.

In Kow Gardons today, a Scotsman with a woodon log was caught hiding in the troos, aftor boing stung on tho knoos by a swarm of boos. Aftor his arrost for indocont oxposure ho statod ho was turning ovor a now loaf and changing his sox.

Sports Nows: Lato rosult: Cholsoa, throo. Loods, ono.

The woathor. Tomorrow's woather will bo wot . . . will be what? Ah . . . will bo wot . . . with a touch of sloot.

Woll, that's all from mo. Ovor now to tho ''Wook in Wostminstor''. Oh God . . . *(Starts to woop . . . . .)*

THO OND

Anyone who's thrilled to the flash of a Kingfisher's wing scudding under Barnes Bridge, while on the way to the shops, and later queued up in the fishmongers behind a load of Kingfishers, knows the fleeting evanescent nature of all that we mortal men enjoy. Where, for example, are the 'trends' of yester-year? Aye where are they? Remember when it was still trendy to be trendy? When a trend in need was a trend indeed? You don't? Oh, knickers!

TRENDS

A party. R.B., very trendily dressed, is chatting to two very trendily dressed girls. Enter R.C. he is very ordinarily dressed. R.C. advances to join the group in a series of hops, both legs together, like a kangaroo.

R.C. Hullo.

R.B. Hullo, glad you could come. Have a drink. *(R.C. takes a drink.)* That's an unusual walk you've got there.

R.C. It's the fashion. It's all the rage. It's the fun thing to do. At least, I thought I read somewhere — I thought I read — isn't it?

R.B. No.

R.C. Oh.

R.B. No, it's utterly ridiculous and nobody does it.

R.C. Oh.

R.B. Yes, it's ridiculurgle and not at all fashionaburgle.

JENNY Oh, *that's* good. I like that. Marvellurgle.

R.B. Yes, it's rather furgle. I thought of it mysurgle.

R.C. I suppose that's a trend, is it? How pathetic! Ending all your words with urgle! What fun is there in that? Walking like a kangaroo's much better. You needn't think that'll ever catch on. *(Laughs. Enter Edward.)*

EDWARD Hullurgle, everyburgle.

R.B. Hullurgle. Have a drurgle.

EDWARD Oh, Thurgle very murgle.

RB *(Indicating drinks)* There's jurgle, whurgle or brurgle.

EDWARD Oh, whurgle, plurgle, and a splurgle of surgle. *(Smiles at R.C.)* Hullurgle.

R.C. Hullo. Pathetic. I mean, really, you're like a lot of shurgle — sheep.

R.B. Perhaps that's just J. Worthington Fitz-sour grapesville.

R.C. What? That's another trend I suppose. Saying J. Worthington Fitz-everything.

R.B. J. Worthington Fitz-exactly.

R.C. How lucky for him! You see, I can be amusing without gimmicks.

R.B. When? *(He leans back, makes camp gesture with limp hands. The others, lined up behind R.B., all follow suit. R.C. stares at them.)*

R.C. 'When?' *(Imitates the gesture.)* Is that another one?

R.B. Yes, everyone's been doing that since, oh, it must be last Tuesday. It was all the rage at Magnus's house warming parturgle.

R.C. *(Imitating)* 'It was all the rage at Magnus's house warming parturgle'.

(R.B. does Groucho Marx walk, with imaginary cigar.)

JENNY Oh that's good. *(They all start doing it.)*

R.C. Well I mean I could do that. I just don't feel like it. *(Makes and noise like a duck.)* Quack.

R.B. I like that. That's rather good. Do it again.

R.C. Do what? Quack.

R.B. I think that's rather fun quack.

R.C. Hells bells. There's no need to make fun of my speech defect quack. Hells bells quack.

R.B. Oh . . er . . I'm sorry. Quack. Well, it's rather good . . and perhaps it'll catch on and then everyone'll be doing it and nobody'll notice that you're doing it. Quack.

OTHERS Quack. Super. Quack.

R.B. If it's a speech defect you ought to go and see a quack doctor.

R.C. What's the use of a quack doctor? I want a real quack doctor. Oh look at the state you've got me in with your stupid trends.

R.B. I'm bored. I want something new.

EDWARD: Magnus'll come up with something nurgle. *(Enter man with beard.)*

BEARD Hullo. Lovely partipoos.

R.B. Rupert! Drinkipoos?

BEARD Pleasipoos. *(Takes a drink. R.C. watches with disgust.)*

R.B. I like your beard. *(Takes beard from pocket, begins to put in on. The others all do the same including the Girls.)* Jenny! That's lovely. Quack. *(Does his camp gesture. Turns to R.C.)* Haven't you got a beard with you?

R.C. No, I . . I've lost mine. No I haven't. I haven't got one, and I don't want one. I'm not interested in fashions. I think that sort of thing's gone out of fashion. *(Enter man in ARP helmet with whistle.)*

ARP MAN *(Blowing whistle)* Everyone in the shelters.

ALL EXCEPT R.C. Everyone in the shelters. Super.

R.B. I thought they might come in again. *(Gets a pile of ARP helmets off a table and begins handing them round.)* I picked them up cheap in 1940, just in case. Oh, I can't wait for Magnus to see all thurgle. *(Makes his camp gesture.)*

R.C. Magnus Schmagnus. *(They all ignore him. They are busy quacking, walking like Groucho Marx, Blowing their whistles, making camp gestures.)* Oh, I'm going Fitzbloodihomipoos and I'm nurgle coming burgle. *(Goes towards door. A handsome tall man stands there. They all stop their activities.)*

ALL Magnus!

R.C. Quack.

MAGNUS: Hullo. *(Hops in, kangaroo style, exactly as R.C. did.)*

R.C. It's back. It's in. It's come back.

MAGNUS: Everyone's doing it at the Cheveleys.

R.B. Let's all go to the Cheveleys.

R.C. Yes let's.

R.B. No, no. You mustn't come. Fashions are out of fashion, you said. You don't rely of gimmicks.

R.C. No . . I . . did I . . well perhaps you're right . . . good-er . . goodbye. Thank you for the party. Quack.
(They all kangaroo out gaily. R.C. bursts into tears. Another man enters. Looks at R.C. R.C. tries to stop.)

MAN Good. I *like* that. *(Bursts into tears also.)*

THE GOVERNMENT SPOKESMAN.
The slicked down hair, the thin municipal moustache,
the air of complete assurance; it's the official
spokesman again. This time he's very deeply into

WATER

SPOKESMAN Good evening. I want to speak to you tonight
about the water shortage. Now there have been rumours
that the Government are washing their hands of the whole
problem. But we're not — because there isn't any water. But
there has been this ridiculous rumour that the cows in the
North East are giving dried milk. Let me deal with that one
straight away. It's true.

How bad is the crisis?

Here's a chart showing Britain's goldfish reserves which have been left high and dry, yes, very dry and extremely high. And it's true that in the annual Upper Thames fishing contest yesterday, the winner caught a seven pound ferret. Indeed on Tuesday, I travelled by train from Manchester to London and I didn't pass water once.

Which brings me to sport.

The water shortage is going to affect sport just a bit. Next week there'll be treacle skiing at Ruislip; the 5th test will be at Henley and the boat race will be at Wimbledon closely followed by tossing the caber and swan-upping, though not necessarily in that order. At Ascot the water will only be turned on on Ladies Day and the ladies will of course be turned on on Water Day.

But what are the Government doing? Well, here's a map that makes it all simple.

And here's the *real* map that makes it look a ghastly mess.

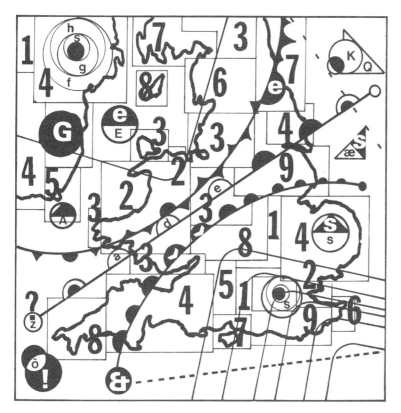

This is the Grand Union Mudbath here and over here the Severn bore will have to be taken up river by lorry, Worcestershire becomes a reservoir — and of course, Waterloo becomes Elsan.

But what can *you* do about it? Firstly you can buy our new economy watering can.

And you know we can't have everyone washing down their cars every Sunday. Do it on a Wednesday. Try to combine going to the toilet with cleaning the windows. If your whisky's too strong, add a drop of gin. And how about making tea without water? Well, here is a teapot. *(Demonstrates)* It's one spoonful per person and one for the pot, shake well and pour yourself a nice cup of tealeaves.

I have to end with an emergency message. It's for girls in the London area. From now on you're asked to share your baths, as only the bathroom at Buckingham Palace will have continuous water. Or to sum up, it's either two pairs or a Royal Straight Flush.

Goodnight.

Ronnie Corbett says there are times when an actor reaches a sticking point in some sketch or play. He gets to the line and, try as he will, he can't pass it without making a mistake. At last he manages it, only to muff the next line. 'The Howling Brothers of St. Wilkinson' is the only sketch in this book that never got transmitted on the show. Ronnie Corbett as the novice monk looked so funny when he came in that things seemed to go slightly wrong from the start. Maybe this is just a writer's excuse. Here is the sketch that never was . . . .

The Howling Brothers of St Wilkinson

The Abbot's cell. It has gothic windows and suggests the ascetic life excepting only that the chair behind the desk looks very comfortable. Many formidable tomes are on the desk. The wind moans. Seagulls cry. Then in the distance we hear the monks chanting plainsong.
The Abbot stands with his back to us, looking out of the window. There is a timid knock at the door.

ABBOT *(Without turning.)* Enter in peace.
(Enter young brother Cyril, obviously a novice, with a new habit and an eager smile.)

CYRIL I'm the new Brother, Father.
(The abbot turns to face the novice and we see that he has a large fat cigar in his mouth. He lays it down on the desk.)

ABBOT Ah, Brother Cyril. So you've decided to renounce the joys of the world and join us?

CYRIL Yes, Father. Oh, it's going to be wonderful here. I'm going to be really miserable.

ABBOT Did you have a good trip from the mainland?

CYRIL Oh yes thank you, Father. I was sick three times.

ABBOT Ah, you mortified the flesh.

CYRIL Well, I mortified my breakfast.

ABBOT Our founder, the Venerable Wilkinson, rowed himself here in a coracle in 1142.

CYRIL 1142! Think of it!

ABBOT Yes, in 11 minutes 42 seconds, and the record still stands. He was sick four times. He brought up three children.

CYRIL Good gracious.

ABBOT He was a mother to them. They became the first monks here. So harsh were the conditions on this island . . . for three years they ate only turnips . . . that every minute of the day upon the minute all the monks howled. Thus we became the 'Howling Order of St. Wilkinson'. Can you howl?

CYRIL Well, I've been practising in the smallest room.

ABBOT How thoughtful. *(Looks at his watch.)* Ah, excuse me. *(Throws back head and howls.)* Ah, that's better out than in.

CYRIL Ah, er, yes . . .*(Clears throat, does pathetic howl.)*
Sorry. I'll practise at night.

ABBOT No howling after 6 p.m.

CYRIL *(Other monks are heard howling from various parts of the monastery.)* Oh.

ABBOT Now, Brother. Do sit down.

CYRIL My feet are killing me.

ABBOT All right. Stand up then.

CYRIL Thank you. I'm really going to renounce the lusts of the flesh like billy-oh.

ABBOT Well said, Brother Cyril. Now you will find your cell furnished only with the bare essentials . . . a bed, a wooden chair, a picture of the founder and a washbasin. And a shower and a low flush toilet. And a fitted cupboard, three piece suite, televison, stereogram, and of course a cocktail cabinet.

CYRIL *(Taken aback.)* Oh! It's more than I expected, father.

ABBOT We rise early here. You will arise for early devotions at the crack of eleven o'clock. After devotions, that'll be five past eleven, you may return to your bed. Lunch is at 1.30. On Sunday however we all have a lie-in.

CYRIL *(Puzzled)* Oh yes, I see.

ABBOT On *no* account may you have a woman in your cell . . .

CYRIL Perish the thought, Father.

ABBOT . . . after midnight. Except on Saturdays and Lady Days. No monkey business during Lent, and *no* jokes of a suggestive nature in the bar till after vespers . . . oh yes, a word about your dirty habits.

CYRIL I'm sorry, Father.

ABBOT They go to the laundry on Tuesdays. *(Glances at watch, throws back head and howls. Cyril follows with a howl rather better than his first one.)*

CYRIL I'm getting the hang of it.
(A comfy lady enters with coffee trolley.)

LADY 'Ello, pet. Coffee?

ABBOT Yes, please, Jackie.

LADY Cream 'n sugar?

ABBOT You spoil me, Jackie.

LADY Chocolate éclair, love?

ABBOT Let's be sinful. *(Takes it and pats her on backside. She squeals.)*

LADY Naughty old Abbot! *(Exits with smile for the very puzzled Cyril.)*

ABBOT Another hardship we have to endure. *(Bites into éclair, looks out of window.)* Generations of holy men have graced this sacred island, down on their knees, toiling ceaselessly with their hands . . there is Brother Onesimus now sweating in the long grass by the refectory . . . I don't know who the girl is . . . *(Turning away)* Well, Cyril, welcome to our order but never forget our Latin tag. Cogito ergo sum hic haec hoc per ardua ad astra in memoriam.

CYRIL What does it mean, Father?

ABBOT I haven't the faintest idea. I have little time for trifles. By the way, would you like this trifle? *(Picks up a small trifle on a paper dish.)*

CYRIL Er, no thank you, Father.

ABBOT Ah.
(He opens an ancient holy book and places the trifle in it. He closes the book with care and wipes off the cream that has been squeezed out of the pages and absent mindedly licks his fingers.)

CYRIL Father, this is terrible.

ABBOT I know. We must get a new cook.
(The Abbot opens a bible revealing a console of switches. He touches a switch and sensuous music begins. The Abbot picks up a scent bottle and puffs at himself. Cyril leaps across and switches off the music.)

CYRIL I can't stand it! I came here for a simple life . . .
(The Abbot glances at his watch. Both men howl in unison. Then Cyril resumes as if nothing had happened.)

CYRIL I came here to deny myself, to deny myself the pleasures of the flesh.

ABBOT Do finish this éclair.

CYRIL No, I don't want it. I mean I do want it but I don't want to want it. I mean I want to stop wanting what I want.

ABBOT *(Standing and towering over the brother in righteous wrath.)* It isn't as simple as that. You foolish vain little monk, what do you know of self denial? You came here because you *enjoy* denying yourself those things. Therefore I tell you that at this monastery you will learn to *deny* yourself that pleasure of denying yourself. From now on your life will be an orgy!!

CYRIL No no! Not the orgy.

ABBOT *(Ringing a hand bell)* Sister Bonaventure! Sister Beatrice! *(Enter two gorgeous girls in fishnet stockings and mini habits.)* Take him away.

CYRIL No, no let me go . . . I didn't understand. I . . . no, not this! *(They take him away struggling.)*

ABBOT Poor boy . . . Just like me when I came here . . . What a hard lonely road . . . *(He takes a whisky and soda from another ancient tome.)* Brother Eustace!
(Enter Brother Eustace, a jolly gay monk laden with garlands and grapes and flagons.)

EUSTACE Hello sailor!

ABBOT Oh miserere! *(He howls. Eustace howls whoopsily. In the distance all the monks howl one by one.)*

63

'Clumsy' was a difficult monologue to perform because on television a little farce goes a long way. I mean, how many custard pies did you see on the nine o'clock news last year? Barely a dozen. Ronnie Barker played the man from the Clumsy Society with perfect seriousness.

Clumsy

Enter R.B. he stumbles over chair — eventually manages to sit down at desk.

R.B. Good evening. I'm appealing to you tonight on behalf of the society for the very clumsy. *(Moves chair forward,. bangs knee against table, winces.)* You know, it can be very unpleasant to be clumsy. Last week one of our members broke 44 bones . . . 9 of them his own. Even I myself do tend to knock over the occasional table . . . in fact last month I knocked over five occasional tables. *(Takes glasses off. Puts them on table.)*

Now our society was founded in the 16th century by the executioner who beheaded Sir Thomas More . . . although he was actually aiming at Anne Boleyn. Today we have 26,000 members . . . you'll be pleased to learn that only 87 of these are in hospital today . . . and even gladder to know that only 53 of these are surgeons.

Two years ago we decided to set up a clumsy centre. Our president, Sir Henry Splint, himself laid our foundation stone with the immortal words: "Ouch. The bloody thing's on my toe." We've also built a school for the children of members of the clumsy society . . . but so far none of them have had any children.

Now here is an appeal box, made by our own hands. *(Holds up very clumsily made box. Puts it down on his glasses. Crunching sound.)* Only one trouble with this box . . . there's no slit to put the money in.

Why do we need your money? For many things. Only ten new pence could keep our members in eggs for two minutes.

We also need special equipment . . . rubber chandeliers, lead greenhouses, balsawood lamp-posts. These things don't grow on trees. and we need to organise expeditions . . . trips abroad, and tumbles at home. *(Pours himself a glass of water . . . Half the water not going in the glass. Tries to mop water away from him across desk as he goes on speaking.)*

Our most successful member is now a very influential butcher. He's got a finger in every pie, but many of our members have to do humdrum jobs like demolition work or managing the British Steel Corporation.

Anyway, do help if you can. Here is our address. *(He pulls down an address roller but it tears off and falls on the floor.)* Never mind, we'll fall off that bridge when we come to it.

Good night.

(He walks smartly off through the scenery.

CHUTE FIRST.

'Chute First' is one of those sketches where the real action takes place offstage. The same thing was true of Hendon Womens' Institute's recent production of 'Ben Hur'. Here, you don't *see* Ronnie Corbett being flung down the laundry chute by the jolly roisterers upstairs, but when he pathetically tries to make light of it, you have to imagine the whole horrible scene . . .

CHUTE FIRST

A hotel basement. Tables. Steam. A large chute upstage. A washing machine. A bag of washing comes down the chute. A man in white overalls (Johnson), picks up the bag, empties out the contents, and puts them in the washing machine.

JOHNSON *(Musing)* Room 317 again. How does he get through so much. Glad he's not staying here long.
More washing down the chute. Procedure as before.

JOHNSON Oh . . . hello. 812. Thought so. She's a bit of a goer. Wasn't like this in the old days. This *was* a four star hotel then.
He goes to the machine. A man (Arkwright), appears down the chute. He gets up, looks around and seeing that Johnson hasn't noticed him, walks off, hurriedly. Johnson comes back to the table, just as another bag descends. He takes out the contents.

JOHNSON Dear, oh dear. What is going on up there? Laundry Room? Piccadilly Circus more like.
He takes the washing to the machine and Arkwright comes down the chute. Johnson turns and sees him.

66

ARKWRIGHT   Evening.

He walks off. Johnson registers slight surprise. He returns to the table. More washing down the chute. One handkerchief this time in a bag.

> JOHNSON   One handkerchief . . . what a liberty. They ought to have a minimum charge.
>
> *He takes it to the machine. Arkwright comes down the chute again. Johnson sees him.*

ARKWRIGHT   Ah! Well, the chute seems to be working all right.

> JOHNSON   Well, it always has. It's a chute innit. Put stuff in the top of a chute, shoots down to the bottom dunnit. That's yer chute.

ARKWRIGHT   Quite. Just checking. Didn't want you to think I'd been flung down it or anything like that. I'm Mr. Arkwright, by the way, the new assistant manager.

> JOHNSON   Johnson — night laundry supervisor.

ARKWRIGHT   Hello. Carry on.
He strides off. Johnson looks askance after him. More washing down the chute. He attends to it.

> JOHNSON   Oh my Gawd . . . all go tonight. All this and a new assistant mana-bloody-ger.
>
> *Arkwright descends.*

ARKWRIGHT   Yes, it definitely is working well.

> JOHNSON   Is someone chucking you down here?

ARKWRIGHT   No, no . . . just tripped on the carpet. Bit of a tuck in it . . . must get that seen to.

> JOHNSON   Who's chucking you down then?

ARKWRIGHT   One of those chaps in 107 . . . you know . . . the Amalgamated Rubber crowd. Having a bit of a party up there.

> JOHNSON   Scotch Mist are they?

ARKWRIGHT   Sorry?

> JOHNSON   Mozart?

ARKWRIGHT   Come again?

> JOHNSON   Legless?

ARKWRIGHT   Oh! Aha!! Well the grape *is* flowing. They are a bit merry.

> JOHNSON   I wouldn't stand for that. Chucking you down the chute and that.

ARKWRIGHT   I won't. Don't you worry. I'm going back up there and I'm going to speak to them pretty straight.

> JOHNSON   Yes, you tell 'em. Reasonable, mind. Diplomatic.

ARKWRIGHT   Yes . . . but I'll be firm.
He exits. More washing for Johnson.

> JOHNSON   Where do they find them? They must have a Useless Twits Training Centre.
>
> *A loud cry off. Arkwright descends.*

ARKWRIGHT . . . or on the other hand . . . more firm than diplomatic, perhaps.

> **JOHNSON** Tell 'em either to knock it off or out they go.

ARKWRIGHT Right! That's the ticket.

> **JOHNSON** But be diplomatic. Tell 'em we're not running an hotel for yobboes.
> *Arkwright exits. He comes down again almost immediately.*

ARKWRIGHT I went in and said: "Excuse me, you types. We want you to have a good time but please remember there are other guests."

> **JOHNSON** I bet that shut 'em up.

ARKWRIGHT Yes, they shut up. Then they picked me up and threw me down the chute.

> **JOHNSON** Well, that's it then innit. Diplomacy has failed . . . tact up the spout. Go in there, all guns blazing.

ARKWRIGHT Right! Le mot juste. I'll go in there with . . . as you so vividly described it . . . all guns . . . as it were . . . blazing. Right!
He exits. More washing for Johnson. He takes out a dress.

> **JOHNSON** Oh Lord . . . him in 427 again.
> *He takes out a picture hat of clashing hue.*

> **JOHNSON** Fancy wearing *that* with that.
> *Arkwright descends. This time with a black eye.*

ARKWRIGHT I think I'm getting through to them. May I

prevail upon you to come up with me for moral support?

THE POST OFFICE.

Did you know that the average British citizen spends 57.8 hours a year queueing in the Post Office? If you've any complaint to make about this disgraceful state of affairs, please write it in triplicate and send it, together with a 5p postal order, which you can obtain at any . . . . . Oh, forget it.

LET'S GO WITH THE G.P.O.!

THE SPOKESMAN Good evening. Many people think the G.P.O. is wasting enormous sums of money — well, I've been paid an enormous sum of money by the G.P.O. to say 'Rubbish' — 'Rubbish!' There, that's money well spent. But seriously you know, we at the G.P.O. are often asked, at a time when we shouldn't be upping prices, why do we up ours? My reply is 'Up yours.'

Now I'd like to tell you about all the wonderful improvements we're making. We know how frustrating it is for you to go into a post office and find that there are only three positions and two of them are closed. So in future all post offices will have twelve positions — and eleven will be closed. And indeed, we're bringing out a new G.P.O. edition of the Kama Sutra. It has 186 positions and 185 of them are closed. But it doesn't end there — Postal services: We are going to *guarantee* two deliveries — March 12th and September 18th.

And we're thinking ahead. Here is our latest stamp design. We've already printed fifty million like this in case a future King of England has a triangular head or Brian Clough becomes Queen, or vice versa.

And by the way, some stamps have come up with a very interesting defect which makes them very valuable. See if you can spot it. *(Shows picture of enormously enlarged 6½p stamp. The stamp is perfect.)* Yes — that's it. Too bloody big to go on the envelope.

Where does this get us? *(The phone on his desk rings with the new squeaky sound.)* Ah! This'll be an important message. Note the new agreeable ringing tone. *(Phone squeaks again.)* This is part of our whole new range of wonderful tones we're introducing. One is so high that only dogs answer it. *(Picks up phone.)* Hello? Damn! They've rung off. Where was I? Today you can dial for almost anything. This morning I dialled for the sports news, the weather and today's recipe. There was a slight crossed line but I can tell you that the South of England will be marinaded in squally showers at twenty minutes a pound at a temperature of 97 for 3, and the outlook is warm with parsley sauce, Regulo 7, West Ham 2.

And now a word about the correct addressing of envelopes. For example, what's wrong with this? *(He holds envelope in his hand and reads from it:)* 'The man with the stupid ears, The house with the revolting curtains, The street with the car parked in it, The town where Tessa was sick, That boring county with all those bloody cows — BX4 7PG . . . *(He now puts up a caption showing the envelope with this exact address on it.)* Yes, you've spotted it! It should be BX4 *8*PG.

(The phone quacks twice. He picks it up.) Hello, ducks?

What's that? No, I am *not* wearing a frilly black nightie, you disgusting pervert! Try Thursday night. *(Puts phone down.)*

Now, parcels. Well, we take great care of parcels. If your parcel is breakable and precious the G.P.O. have to mark it fragile. *(He takes a small delicate parcel in mauve paper with a ribbon and smashes it with a huge rubber stamp, totally destroying it.)*

Now this is the new Common Market standard parcel. *(He demonstrates a 12'' cube.)* From now on all parcels must be this size and shape. You'll be surprised how much you can send. Here's a football. *(Shows cube shaped football.)* Here's an ostrich's egg. The ostrich is as well as can be expected.

And this of course is a Common Market bicycle wheel. *(Holds up square bicycle wheel.)*

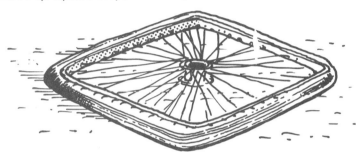

Where does this get us? Well, not very far unless the roads are icy . . . *(A cow moos. He looks round then realises it's the new G.P.O. phone. He looks at it then hits it with a hammer. It squeaks and dies.)*

Lastly, the problem of unwanted mail. A lady in Brondesbury writes, "I'm worried. Today I received a very frank pamphlet entitled 'Seven Ways of Getting Pregnant' through my letter box . ." Well, Mrs. S. we've tried and there are only *three* ways of getting pregnant through your letter box — so keep your pecker up. Oh! That's four ways!

Well there you have it. If you want to send your new born baby a telegram for his hundredth birthday — start queueing *now*.

Goodnight.

CLIFFHANGER

Peter Robinson is remarkable for two things. Firstly his name is the same as that of a well known store which shall be nameless. And secondly he wrote this sketch.

Ronnie Barker enters his office on the 16th floor, deposits bowler, brief case and brolly, moves to open window, and studies his Financial Times for a few moments. He casually glances out of window, sees Ronnie Corbett hanging from sill by his fingertips.

R.B.   Good morning.

R.C.   *(Smiles shyly)* Hullo.

R.B.   Lovely day.

R.C.   Yes.

R.B.   I see Consolidated Steel's up five points.

R.C.   Really?

R.B.   How long have you been hanging there?

R.C.   Oh, about two or three minutes I suppose.

R.B.   Do that sort of thing a lot do you?

R.C.   No, it's my first time actually.

R.B.   I prefer golf myself.

R.C.   Oh, it's not a hobby.

R.B   Isn't it?

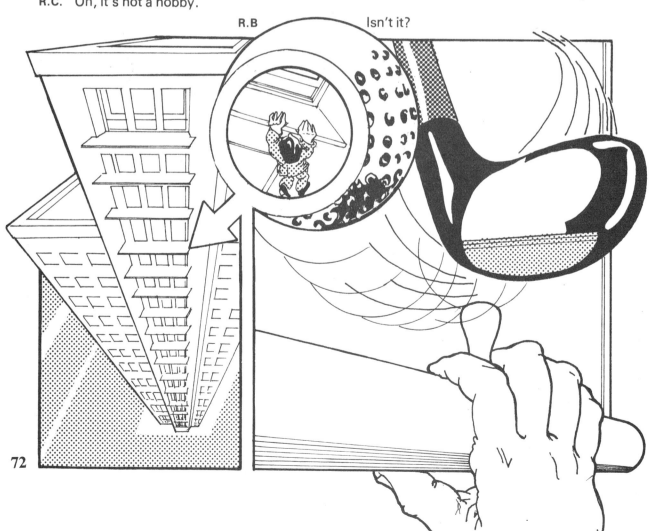

R.C. No, you see, I was leaning out of my window, directly above yours, having a look at our window box, when my secretary, quite unbeknownst to me, came up behind me, and put her hand on my convolvulus.

R.B. Must have given you a shock.

R.C. Yes, it did rather. Before I could say "What the hell d'you think you're doing Naomi, coming up behind me like that and touching my convolvulus, you should have more sense, after all you came to me with five A levels and a lisp", I'd lost my balance and fallen out.

R.B You're lucky to have a secretary who arrives on time — mine's always late.

R.C. Yes, I suppose I am really.

R.B. And then again, you were lucky to grab hold of the ledge here. It really is your lucky day isn't it?

R.C. That's true.

R.B. Still, that's life I suppose.

R.C. C'est la vie.

R.B. La vie.

R.C. Pardon?

R.B. You said say la vie.

R.C. No, c'est la vie. It's a French expression — from France.

R.B. Oh. Oh well can't stand here gossiping all day. Work to do and all that. Enjoyed our little chat. *(He turns away.)*

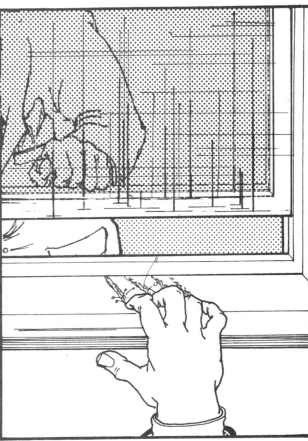

R.C. I say.

R.B. I beg your pardon?

R.C. Could you help me in? Sorry to be a nuisance.

R.B. I'm afraid nobody gets into my office without an appointment.

R.C. Couldn't you make an exception?

R.B I'm sorry, but if I let you in, then others will start drifting in willy nilly, and before you know it my office will be like Euston Station.

R.C. I wouldn't tell anybody.

R.B. You wouldn't have to, these things get about. I have to be very careful, after all, I am the Managing Director.

R.C. Yes, I know. I work for you in accounts — sir.

R.B. Do you really? Thought I recognised your face. Worked for me long have you?

R.C. Five years sir. I might not be here much longer though.

R.B. No, I see what you mean. Still, don't feel too badly about it. Accounts is overstaffed anyway.

R.C. I don't think I shall be able to give the statutary month's notice I'm afraid.

R.B. Don't worry about that old chap. What d'you think I am, a machine? Underneath this rough exterior beats a heart of pure granite.

R.C. That's a relief.

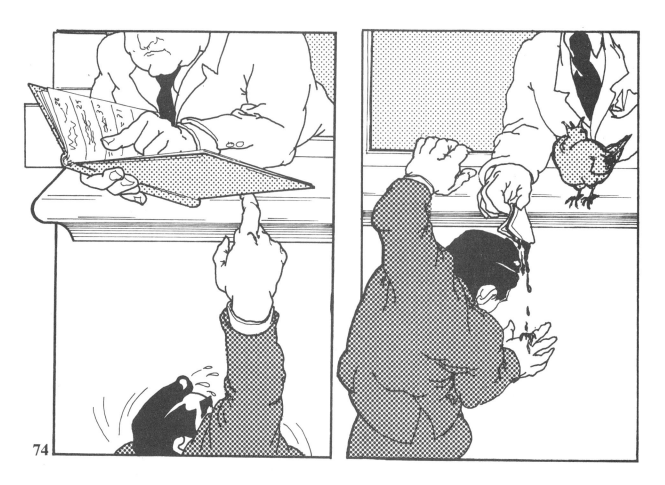

R.B. Pension and insurance contributions all paid up, are they?

R.C. Oh yes.

R.B. Good. Of course, you'll have some leave to come you know.

R.C. I doubt if I'll have time to use it sir.

R.B. I happen to know a company that do lightning tours of the Cairngorms, Urals, and Neasden High Street —? Oh well, I'll say bon voyage then.

R.C. There is one thing sir . . . . .

R.B. Well, go on, speak up man.

R.C. Well, I know it's an awful cheek, but would you mind going up to room 803? There are some pills on my desk. I suffer from hay fever you see, and with the rush of air when I'm falling I might sneeze a bit. Be awfully distracting for people in the offices below. Hope you don't mind me asking.

R.B. Of course I don't mind. Good Lord, what are we here for if it's not to help each other?

R.C. Thank you so much.
(R.B. leaves.)

R.C. *(Calls)* Cynthia!

CYNTHIA *(Emerges from cabinet.)* Oh, I thought you'd never get rid of him. *(She helps him in and they embrace.)*

R.C. You'll have to change your boss dear, that's the third time this week.

PROPS.

The BBC props department regularly work wonders. Those lads could run up a giant carrot or a pair of iced underpants as quickly and easily as you or I could create Stonehenge in fudge. They certainly deserve some sort of monument, though of course if they're going to make it, who's going to afford it? But seriously, folks, in the next piece, "Tomorrow's Kitchen" written by Ian Davidson, which depended on a lot of silly props — they played a blinder. Is that O.K., fellers?

TOMORROW'S KITCHEN

The spokesman stands in somewhat streamlined looking kitchen.

SPOKESMAN Good evening. And welcome to 'The Day After Tomorrow's World' — Tonight we show you something smooth, streamlined, functional and good looking — but that's enough about me. I'm standing in the 'kitchen of the future', the kitchen that's got every labour saving device you can think of apart from the Liberal Party. Ha ha.

Let's look around shall we? *(Points to grill about two foot from the floor.)* First, here's the eye level grill — designed by Ronnie Corbett — and then this one multi-unit combines the mixer, the oven and the washing machine all in one. How does it work?

(Moves to work surface.) Well, supposing I want to make a nice bit of crumpet — well supposing I do? What I do after five o'clock is my business. What about a cake for my birthday? I'll need some cake mix. *(Takes small box.)* This is for short cake. And this is for very long cake. *(Takes long box.)* This one I think. *(Throws whole box into mixing bowl.)* Add the eggs. *(Puts pack of six eggs in bowl.)* Milk. *(Puts milk bottle in bowl.)* Icing sugar. *(Another packet.)* And of course the twenty-one candles. *(Adds a box and an extra candle.)* Mix for only a few seconds. *(Stir the ingredients with wooden spoon.)* And simply pop in the oven.

But remember, this oven and mixer is also the washing machine and I'm doing my laundry. So what do we get? Ouch! Well, first we get an electric shock. Now to time the cooking — let's check the digital clock. *(He opens a small cupboard and is presented with a two finger sign.)*

Either it's two o'clock or they're still on strike. While the cake's doing, what about the food of the future? Well we scientists have found that the old traditional vegetables are too small. What for example can I do with this carrot? *(Holds up standard carrot.)* Thank you very much, Madam. Well, I tried them first as a decoration. I gave my wife this eighteen carrot ring.

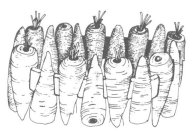

And she divorced me. But that's not enough — here is one single section from the super carrot of the future. *(Takes section of carrot about two feet across.)*

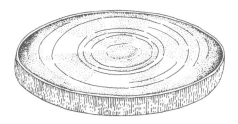

If you ate the whole of this side you'd turn bright orange and everybody could see you in the dark and on *this* side there's Matt Monro singing 'I'm in the Mood for Love' — and with all that vitamin I'm not surprised.

Now here's the new BBC radish. *(Shows giant radish.)*

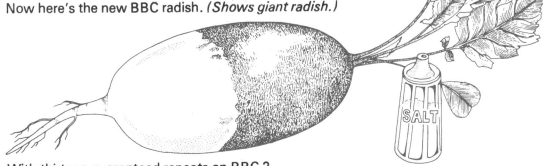

With thirteen guaranteed repeats on BBC 2.

And here's an oven ready budgerigar. *(Shows huge turkey. A telephone rings. He picks up a large cucumber.)* Hello? Sorry, wrong cucumber.

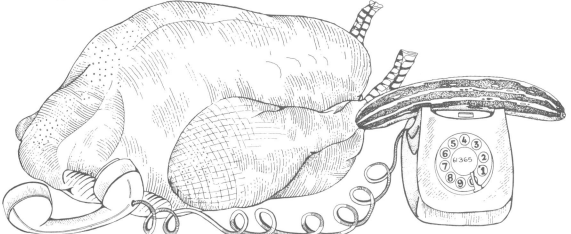

But what about pests in the kitchen? Here is the mousetrap of the future. It consists of a piece of cheese, a Jimmy Young record and a brick. When the mouse smells the cheese he comes out of his hole. Play the Jimmy Young record and when the poor little so and so puts his paws over his ears you creep up behind him and clobber him with the brick. Simple really.

But where is the chicken of the future? Well she's in this illuminated box. She's a battery chicken. Ha ha. What about feeding her then? In this pellet there's enough concentrated chicken food for six months. I load it into a special gun and by means of this aperture I can shoot the pellet straight into her mouth, thus. *(He fires the gun. There is a dreadful squawk from the box.)* Sorry. Wrong end.

Now the cake should be ready . . . *(Takes it out of oven.)* Here we are, a very nice cake in wool rayon mixture with a zip front — and a fine pair of iced underpants. *(Removes stiffened underpants which are iced and have twenty-one candles burning on top.)*

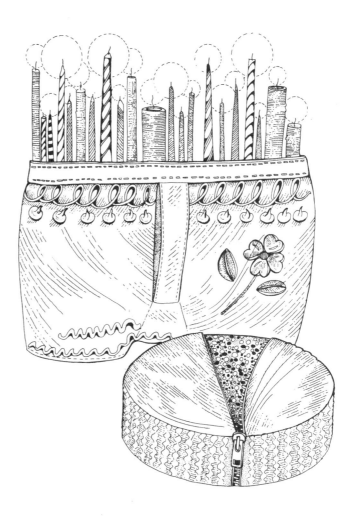

Well, tonight there'll be a following wind and a cold front. Goodnight.

THE SHOOTING SCRIPT.
When a script arrives from the writer it is in pristine
condition save for the odd patch of blood, sweat and
tears. When the director's had a go at it, it ends up
looking like this:

ACTION

"PARTY NAMES" (David Nobbs)

84.
4
WS room
RC/JANET in f/g (A PARTY IN PROGRESS.   THE BELL
RINGS.   RC ANSWERS THE DOOR.
RB AND CYNTHIA ARE THERE.)

85.
1
RC/RB/CYNTHIA at door
Pan them L. and
hold 4-sh. as JANET   RC:
joins them from L.   Ah come in.   This is my sister Janet.
Easy to remember, she looks as if she comes
from another planet.   Now you must be ....

86.
4
CS RB

87.
5   RB:
Tight 2-sh RB/RC   Walter.
fav. RC

RC:
Of course.   Dreadful business remembering
names.   Walter's easy, though.   It rhymes
with Malta and I was laid up there for
six weeks with kidney trouble.

88.
4
2-sh RB/CYNTHIA

89.
5   RB:
CS RC   And this is Cynthia Getlost.

RC:
Glad to meet you, Miss Getlost.   I'm Neil.

90.
1   Lean backwards.
4-shot

91.
5   RB:
CS RC   Oh all right.   (THEY DO)

RC:
No, no.   I'm Neil.   That's Lien if you say

92.
4   it backwards.
2-sh RB/CYNTHIA

RB:
Oh I see.   And we thought ... how funny.
(THEY LAUGH)
CYNTHIA:
We were quite taken aback.   (THEY LAUGH AGAIN)

93.
1
4-shot
Tighten to 3-sh
as RC leaves R.

(4 next)

ACTION   SOUND

"PARTY NAMES" (continued)

RC:
Now what will you have to drink?
(DOORBELL GOES) Excuse me. (HE GOES TO THE DOOR)

RB:
Lovely time of year for the weather.

CYNTHIA:
Yes.

JANET:
Lovely.   (THEY LAUGH. NEIL JOINS THEM, BRINGING PERCY AND ALISON)

94.   4
Single RC
immediately developing
to 3-sh with
Percy/Alison
(if too quick 3-sh
all the time)

RC:
Sorry to interrupt the gay chitter chatter but I'd like you all to meet Percy Drophead and Alison Pinrut.

95.
CMS RB

RB:
I say, that's Turnip backwards (LAUGHS)

96.   1
Group shot

RC:
That's easy to remember, then.   Now this is Janet, Malta .....

97.   5
CMS RB

RB:
Walter.

98.   4
Tight RB/RC fav RC

RC:
Malta is very nice at this time of the year and as I was about to say this is Walter, and this is Cynthia .... er ....

99.   5
CMS Cynthia

CYNTHIA:
Getlost.

100.   4
MCU RC

RC:
(SHOCKED) I beg your pardon. (REALISES THAT IT'S HER NAME.) Oh I see (NEIL & CYNTHIA LAUGH)

101.   1
W.S.

(4 next)

ACTION

"PARTY NAMES" (continued)

102.   4
      CMS RC

RB:
Where's Belinda?

RC:
She's in the conservatory, resting.

103.   5
      CMS RB

She's pregnant, you know.

104.   4
      CMS RC

RB:
Really?   How long has she been pregnant?

105.   1
      W.S.
Hold group shot as
RC leaves

RC:
About 20 minutes - that's why she's resting.

Now what will you have to ... (DOORBELL
RINGS) Excuse me. (GOES TO DOOR - AWKWARD
PAUSE)

106.   5
      CMS RB

RB:
Er ... er/ lovely time of year, for the time

107.   1
      W.S.

of year. I mean lovely weather for the
weather.

JANET:
Yes, lovely.

(CYNTHIA SUDDENLY BECOMES OVERCOME WITH
LAUGHTER)

CYNTHIA:
(POINTING AT ALISON) Turnip backwards.

(NEIL ENTERS WITH ALAN)

108.   4
      2-sh RC/Alan

RC:
Sorry to cut in on the merry banter, but
I'd like you all to meet my best and oldest
friend ... er ... er .....

ALAN:
Hiker. Alan Hiker H.I.K.E.R.

(1 next)

(on 1)

"PARTY NAMES" (continued)

RC:
Of course. Like Alan Whicker without the

W.C. / Alan, this is Malta.

109. 1
      W.S.

110. 5
      CMS RB

RB:
Walter.

111. 4
      Tight 2-sh RB/RC   RC:
      fav RC   Yes, of course. I get muddled because I

                           was in kidney for six weeks with Malta trouble.

112. 5
      Tight 2-sh RB/RC
      fav RB   RB:
                           Trouble with the old Maltaworks, eh. (LAUGHS)

113. 1
      W.S.
                           Lovely time of weather for the year.

                           RC:
                           Now, what will you .... (DOORBELL RINGS)

                           Excuse me. / Carry on with the introductions,

114. 4
      Tight 2-sh fav RC   will you, kidney?
      a/b

115. 1
      W.S.
                           RB:
                           On - er - all right. Er - Alan, this is
                           planet from another Janet, Percy Drophead,
                           Alison - er - pinsrap. That's parsnip
                           backwards.

                           CYNTHIA:
                           Turnip.

116. 5
      CMS RB
                           RB:
                           Sorry Alison Turnip. That's Pinrut backwards.

                           (RE ENTER NEIL WITH A SCOTSMAN AND A RUSSIAN
                           GIRL)

117. 1
      W.S.
                           RC:
                           Sorry to break up the jolly old cut and thrust
                           but I'd like you all to meet the Laird of
                           Lifersauchie and Miss Olga Olgina Olivechenka.
                           Have an olive, Miss Olivechenka. (LAUGHS)

84

(5 next)

ACTION

(on 1)

"PARTY NAMES" (continued)

RC: (continued)
Now this is Alison Turnip backwards, Alan
Whicker. Alan, Alison, meet the Laird of
Lifersauchie. (THEY SHAKE HANDS) This
is Cynthia Petmost.

118. 5
      ‾‾‾‾
      CS RC   PERCY:
                               Getlost.

RC:
(FURIOUS AT WHAT HE TAKES TO BE A RUDE
REMARK) Drop dead.

119. 1
      ‾‾‾‾
      W.S.   PERCY:
                               Drophead.   Percy Drophead.

                               RC:
                               Have an olive, Miss Planet.

                               JANET:
                               Are they stuffed?

120. 4
      ‾‾‾‾‾‾
      MCU RC   RC:
                               No, you eat them. / (DOORBELL RINGS) Excuse
121. 1
      ‾‾‾‾   me.   Carry on with the introductions, will
      W.S.
                               you ... er ... er ... (GOES TO THE DOOR)

                               RB:
                               (GETTING MORE AND MORE CONFUSED) Yes. Er -
                               this is Janet.   Janet, meet Olga Olge Olga -
                               Olga. / Olga, meet the Laird of Liversausage,
122. 5   W.C. Hiker, Alison Brastrap, Percy Thrower.
      ‾‾‾‾‾
      CS RB   Percy, meet Olga recurring.   Oh you two
                               know each other. / (LAUGHS NERVOUSLY)

123. 4   Now I'm - er. Who am I?
      ‾‾‾‾‾‾‾‾‾‾‾‾‾‾
      2-sh RB/Cynthia

                               CYNTHIA:
                               Walter.

(1 next)   85

ACTION

(on 4)

"PARTY NAMES" (continued)

RB:
And this is my fiancee - er - er

CYNTHIA:
(ANGRILY) Cynthia Getlost.

RB:
My fiancee, Cynthia Getlost.   That's
Hotlegs backwards.

124.   1
        W.S.   (RE ENTER NEIL WITH A GERMAN)

RC:
Sorry in dampen the intellectual ebb and flow,
everyone, but I'd like you to meet Count Von
Essel of Graeben.   Now what will you .../

125.   4
        CS RC   (DOORBELL RINGS) Excuse me.   (GOES TO DOOR)
Do the introductions, Waterworks.

RB:
Er - er - lovely - er - this is Cynthia
Hotlegs, Alison Dropout,/Percy Potato, Alan

126.   5
        CS RB   Toilet Recurring, Vanessa Redgrave.   This
is Stuffed Olga, and the lump of Liversausage.
I'm kidney parsnips from Malta. (STOPS IN
TOTAL CONFUSION)

127.   1
        W.S.   (ENTER NEIL WITH THREE POLICEMEN)

P.C. POTTS:
Hullo hullo hullo hullo.

GUESTS:
(POLITELY) Hullo hullo hullo hullo.

P.C. POTTS:
There's a lot of cars double parked outside.

128.   4
        Tight 2-sh RC/PC POTTS

(1 next)

(on 4)

"PARTY NAMES" (continued)

RC:
Just who do you think you are bursting in
on me like this?

P.C. POTTS:
Oh, I'm sorry. I'm P.C. Potts,/this is

129.   1
        W.S.   P.C. White and P.C. Chambers.

RC:
Alison, Vanessa, Malta, Kidney, meet P.C.s
White Chamber Potts. I'm Neil. Lean
backwards.
(THEY ALL BEGIN AN ORGY OF INTRODUCTIONS,
HAND SHAKING, LEANING BACKWARDS, ETC.)

RECORDING PAUSE

BOFFO

Ronnie Barker is at desk. Some products in front of him and some more products on a few shelves behind him.

RONNIE Good evening, or, if you live on the Great Barrier Reef, good middle of the night. And welcome to Consumer's Corner. Last week we tested twelve different kinds of glue. I said that 'Boffo' glue was best, and I'm sticking to it. Now certain people have bandied it about that I favour Boffo products because I am paid by them. What rubbish! People like that ought to be boiled in oil. And I recommend 'Boffo' oil.

Let's start this week with cornflakes. Here is the 'Boffo' pack. *(Produces huge packet of cornflakes labelled 'Boffo')* And here is another make. *(Produces normal sized pack marked 'Another make')* As you can see, Boffo is much bigger. Doesn't this make it heavy to carry? I hear some idiot ask. Well, Boffo have thought of that — so it's three quarters empty. Then why not a smaller pack? Boffo have thought of that, too — and here it is, inside the larger pack. *(Produces normal size pack from inside larger pack.)* And just look at the cornflakes! *(Produces one immense cornflake.)*

It's but a short step from cornflakes to transistor radios for the pocket. Two new makes this week. One Japanese — *(Produces radio about the size of a cigarette pack.)* The other is this one. *(Produces huge clumsy ugly radio.)* And it's British! This is the one for my money. Who could lose that? Let's see who makes it! *(Turns it round. It says 'Boffo' across the back.)* What a coincidence! Yes, Boffo make the world's largest miniature radio. And another selling point. *(Turns it on. A barely audible crackle is heard.)* — you can hardly hear it. So no complaints from the neighbours.

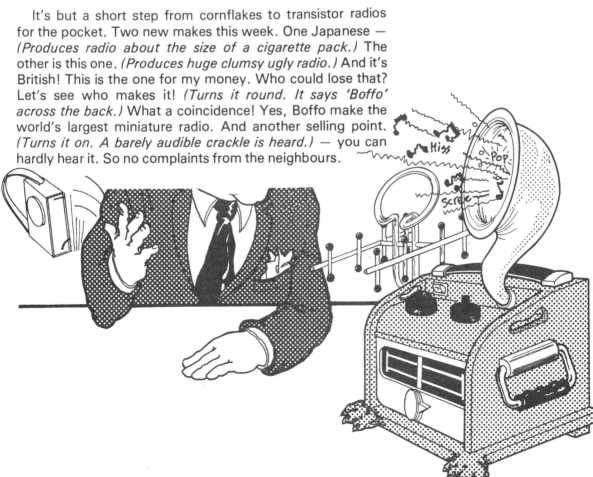

(Taking a packet of dried risotto) There's no bias in my tests on foodstuffs. For instance *every* firm must list the contents on the package. Let's take one at random. What's this? *(Looks at packet.)* 'Boffo Beef Risotto' Mmm. Sounds good. *(Reads)* ''Contains beef substitute, vegetable substitute, rice substitute, edible spices, inedible spices, monosodium glutamate substitute, and a rusty nail''. Well, you can't get much fairer than that — unless you dye your hair with Boffolene hair dye, or use Boffo hair restorer, as I did on this billiard ball. *(Holds up billiard ball with growth of six inch hair all over top.)*

Last week I asked you to let me know what you would like me to test next. 78% replied 'Balls'. Well, here is a 'Boffo' Beach Ball. *(Bounces a rubber ball.)* And here is a crystal ball. *(Drops it in same way. It shatters.)* No more need be said.

Earlier today I washed two identical shirts, one with Boffo Blue, with the secret ingredient, and one with a cheese grater. *(Produces the cheese grater.)* Here is the shirt washed with the cheese grater. *(Holds up shredded shirt.)* But here, on the other hand, is the shirt washed with Boffo. *(Produces an equally shredded shirt.)* Yes — three shades whiter!

I also made a strictly impartial cooking test — monitored by a neutral observer, the Managing Director of Boffo. I took two different products, a Boffo Chicken Curry and a large stone. I cooked each of them for twenty minutes at gas number 7 — and here is the result. *(Produces plate with chicken chips and peas.)* Here is the Boffo chicken curry, chips and peas. A Welsh housewife tasted it and pronounced it: *(Welsh accent)* 'Chicken curry chips and peas' — on the other hand here is the large stone, chips and peas. *(Produces a a large stone, chips and peas on a plate. He bangs the stone with a fork.)* You see? Still extremely tough.

And here's a bit of news! This week every single Boffo product costs 45% less. 45% less than what? 45% less than it will cost next week.

Well, I'll finish, as always with our shoppers' weather guide. *(Goes to weather map which has two large 'O's, one over west Britain, one over east Britain.)* As you can see there are two depressions. But in the midlands it will be fairly foggy. *(Puts 'FF' on the map between the two 'O's.)* While Western districts will be affected by Hurricane Bertha. *(Puts a 'B' in front of the 'OFFO'.)* So there it is, Boffo! It's a *good* buy. Goodbye.

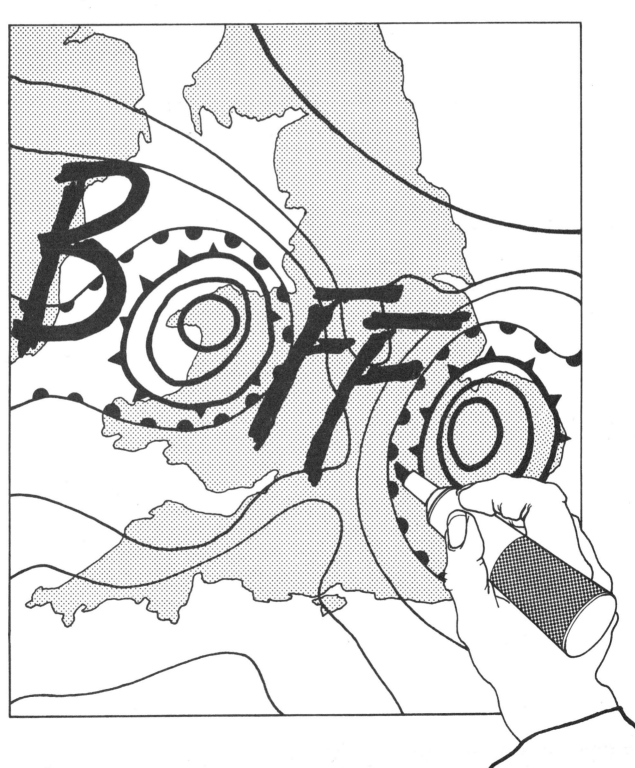

POST HYPNOTIC SUGGESTION

Party scene. Smart people. Girls include an elegant coloured girl and a member of the WRNS.

HENRY Hello George! Good to see you! Have a sausage roll.

GEORGE *Atishoo!*

HENRY Oh dear . . or a gherkin.

GEORGE *Atishoo!*

HENRY Bless you!

GEORGE No . . sorry but whenever you mention food I sneeze.

HENRY Oh dear well . . . *(Raising his drink)* Here's to getting better! Let's drink a toast!

GEORGE *Atishoo!*

HENRY Oh sorry! I said toast didn't I?

GEORGE *Atishoo!*
    You're just making fun of me! People are looking now. For heaven's sake man . . . . . where's your breeding?

HENRY Breeding?? I'm extremely well bred.

GEORGE Bread? *Atishoo!*

HENRY Sorry!

GEORGE Look I'm sorry I snapped at you, but it happened when I went to that hypnotism show. The 'Great Mysto'. He put me under . . . you know — just for a lark . . .

HENRY *Cockadoodledoo!*

GEORGE What?

HENRY Sorry, I do that whenever anyone mentions a bird. And you said L.A.R.K.

GEORGE L.A.R.K.? Oh! Lark!

HENRY *Cockadoodledoo!*
    Oh dear . . . yes I went to the Great Mysto too . . he hypnotised *me.*

GEORGE Well he's coming to this party so he can cure us.

HENRY Yes, and meanwhile, George, since people are

looking round at us, let's not mention food or birds.

GEORGE   Right.

HENRY   Right. *(Pause)*

GEORGE   Still we must talk a bit. We mustn't be chicken!

HENRY   *Cockadoodledoo!*

GEORGE   *Atishoo!*   *(Together)*

GEORGE   Oh this is awful, let's talk to someone else and forget all about it.

HENRY   Right.

GEORGE   *(Calling)* Er . . . Robin!

HENRY   *Cockadoodledoo!*

GEORGE   Oh I'm so sorry . . er Ro . . . er Ro*bert.* This is Ro*bert.*

ROBIN   Robert??

GEORGE   Yes. You're Ro*bert.* Meet Robert Vulture.

HENRY   *Cockadoodledoo!*

GEORGE   Sorry sorry!

ROBIN   How do you do . . er have you met my girlfriend?

GEORGE   Oh which is your girlfriend. Is it the Wren?

HENRY   *Cockadoodledoo!* . . *Please!*

ROBIN   No. It's the black bird.

HENRY   *Cockadoodledoo!*
Oh dear . . . This really takes the biscuit!

GEORGE   *Atishoo!*

HENRY   Gesundheidt!

ROBIN   *Booooom!*

OTHERS   What??

ROBIN   Sorry. I went to this hypnotist . . .

OTHERS   The Great Mysto?

ROBIN   Yes, and whenever I hear a German word I go *Boom*

GEORGE   Well we should be able to avoid that one! Drink anyone?

HENRY   No thanks. I've got my bitter . . .

ROBIN   *Booooom!* Oh nuts . . .

GEORGE   *Atishoo!*

HENRY   Gesundheidt . . no *not gesundheidt!*

ROBIN   *Boom Boom!*
Sorry . . . oh I feel such a peasant.

HENRY *Cockadoodledoo!*

GEORGE He said *peasant* not pheasant!

HENRY *Cockadoodledoo!*

GEORGE Sorry.

GIRL *(Passing their group)* *Wheeeee!*

ALL THREE What's the matter?

GIRL Oh dear, well, I went to this hypnotist . . .

OTHERS The Great Mysto —

GIRL Whenever I hear an apology I go *Wheeeee!*

HENRY How very inconvenient.

GEORGE We won't apologise then.

HENRY No we'll keep right off all awkward things.

GEORGE Once bitten eh?

ROBIN Bitter? *Booooom!*

GEORGE No I said 'bitten'.

HENRY Bittern?? *Cockadoodledoo!*

ROBIN No he said 'bitten' as in 'I have bitten the scone . . .'

GEORGE *Atishoo!*

ROBIN Oh sorry!

GIRL *Wheeeee!*

OTHERS Oh sorry!

GIRL *Wheeeee!*

GEORGE Look we really must stop all this . . .

OTHERS Yes.

GEORGE: Er . . lovely weather we're having . . I think?

OTHERS Yes.

GEORGE Not a bird in the sky.

OTHERS No.

GEORGE Nor any food or Germans or apologies.

OTHERS No.

GEORGE Good.

HENRY *(Looking happy).* There we are then, a piece of cake! NO!!

GEORGE *Atishoo!*

HENRY I do beg your pardon — NO I DON'T!

GIRL *Wheeeee!*

GEORGE He didn't mean it . . . er . . . er . . . er *(To Henry).* How many er children do you have?

HENRY Nine.

ROBIN   Nein?? *Booooom!*

HENRY   Sorry!

GIRL   *Wheeeee!*

HENRY   Oh *beans!*

GEORGE   *Atishoo!*

HENRY   Sorry.

GIRL   *Wheeeee!*

ROBIN   Why don't you all shut up!

GEORGE   Keep your hair on.

ROBIN   Herr? *Booooom*

GEORGE   Oh . . . let's watch the telly . . .

HENRY   What's on?

OTHERS   'Budgie'.

HENRY   *Cockadoodledoo!*

GEORGE   Sorry.

GIRL   *Wheeeee!*

(The Great Mysto enters.)

MYSTO   Ah my friends!

ALL   The Great Mysto!!

GEORGE   He's come to cure us!

MYSTO   No no. I have given up hypnotism. I can't cure you. Sorry. But I've brought some cold partridge and apple strudel!!

ALL

Wheeeee!
Cockadoodledoo!
Atishoo! Wheeeee!
Booooom! Atish
Atishoo! Coc
Cockadoodlec
Booooom!
Wheeee
Booo

POLLUTION

THE SPOKESMAN Good evening. I'm from the Ministry of Pollution. Now a lot of people say to me 'You're not doing enough about pollution' and I say 'Rubbish', and they say 'You're not doing enough about rubbish' and I say 'Pollution'.

Now to give you an example of our work. We have selected an area for the disposal of toxic waste . . . and here it is — Great Britain. *(He puts down a map of Britain, covered in black marks indicating the big towns).* And we're going to divide Britain into two regions . . . East of Sewage and West of Sewage.

I expect you're wondering what these black marks are. Well they represent big towns. *(Indicates the marks as he speaks.)* That's London, Birmingham, Manchester, and the spot where my wife threw the ink at me. Let's see what happens in 20 years' time. *(Pulls down another map, almost*

As you can see, London is twice as big, Birmingham three times as big, and the spot where my wife threw the ink at me has a population of two million.

Of course certain towns will have to be joined together. For instance, Bognor Regis will join Lyme Regis and be known as Regis Regis, West Ham will join East Sandwich to form two towns known as "West East" and "Ham Sandwich", Staines will join Underhill and be known as Under-Staines, and Southampton will join Northampton and become one enormous Hampton. And there'll be 4 Liverpools, 3 Exeters and of course 2 Bristols.

But we can't fight pollution without some hardship. Certain things will have to be rationed . . . air, for instance. You'll be able to breathe, but not as often as you used to. There'll be a rota system as follows. Glasgow Monday, Leeds Tuesday, Sheffield Wednesday. London will breathe in on Thursdays and out on Saturdays. Sorry, Hastings, your day is February 29th.

Now we are trying to fight the menace of noise. Rowlocks, I hear you say. Well of course they do squeak. But what about supersonic bangs? Well, they're not good for you so don't try it in Concorde. But if we *do* abolish Concorde we'll provide an alternative. A fleet of little men on bicycles will rush round the country making nasty smells and breaking all the stained glass windows . . . and we'll pay them a million pounds a week.

Some people worry about over-population. Well we are dealing with this. In fact in Northumberland, due to a mistake, we have just sterilised all the milk and pasteurised all the men. This means there'll be no half pint bottles and lots of lovely babies with gold tops.

As for living space, we calculate that by 1995 everyone will have two square feet. Which will make walking impossible, so the pavements won't be crowded.

However we are bringing in a new law to help cut down the population. Sex will only be permitted to people whose names begin with X. Sorry.

So there it is. If you've a problem, write to me . . . Mr. James Xbrown *(Caption reveals name . . . 'James Xbrown')* . . . yes, *I'm* all right . . . at this address. 17 Old Bicycle Street, Mattress Garden City, Ashton Under Slime, Rusty Bedsteadshire.

So here's to the future. Cheers. Join me in a slice of water. *(Removes slice of water from glass with a knife.)* Good night. *(Drinks. Grimaces. Dies.)*

GOLOSCHNIK RESTAURANT

(Smart sports-car-set couple arriving in primitive little restaurant. The decor suggests the wilder parts of the Balkans.)

MAN This is the only Goloschnik restaurant in London.

GIRL I've never heard of Goloschnia.

MAN Nor had I but I had this four months off in the Summer, so I thought why not skip the usual boring old places, Samarkand, Tashkent, Vladivostok, the fish and chips belt — and I found myself way up in the mountains in this dinky little place, Goloschnia . . . and you know, the people are heaven!

(Enter waiter, fierce wild looking man with murderous moustache, shaggy clothes, many knives stuck in belt. Like an Albanian brigand with waiterly additions.)

MAN Ah! Hello!

(The waiter glares at him, draws knife and sweeps crumbs of table with it. He hands man primitive-looking menu.)

MAN Ah thank you. Now what about some of this? I first tried this in a little bistro in the Blotz Mountains. Absolutely delicious.

GIRL If you say so . . .

MAN This is the one for us!

WAITER Schkoiz. *(He turns menu up the other way.)*

MAN Ah. Well, yes . . . that's another way of looking at things . . . Ah yes, I can't quite remember what this was — Oosh bolocki . . . ?

WAITER Eesa . . . ees a . . . ees a piece of oosh with bolocki.

MAN Of course! I remember it now. It's a . . . spot of 'oosh' with er bolocki.

GIRL Oh good.

MAN Super. Yes. Twice . . . er two. *(Is about to put two fingers up.)* Oh. Better not. It's one and another one. *(Holds up a finger from each hand.)*

WAITER Aaaaagh! Two! *(Holds up two fingers in man's face then calls through hatch.)* Ooshbolocki. Toop! And to followink?

MAN Ah . . . and 'to followink' *(Flicking vaguely through menu.)* Ah yes, for me — 'Kramlock'.

WAITER Ha! Kramlock! Eez custom! *(Kisses girl.)*

GIRL Do you mind?

MAN Ah! Ha ha . . . It's an old custom I think. They kiss you when you say 'Kramlock'.

WAITER Kraamlock! Yaaz! *(Kisses girl more passionately.)*

GIRL Oh please!

WAITER Thank you.

MAN Er er . . . well I'll have Poofki.

WAITER Poofki! Old custom! *(Tries to kiss man.)*

MAN On second thoughts . . . I won't, thank you. *(Cowbells sound.)*

WAITER Schkoiz. *(Collects two oosh bolockis from hatch. They are octopus tentacles on dish of gherkins. All the dishes are rather large, look suitable for four people rather than one.)*

GIRL *(Doubtfully.)* Oh. Mmmm.

MAN Yes. Mmmmm. *(Sniffs it, gets revolting smell.)* Euuuuurgh!

WAITER *(Delighted.)* You *like!* *(Bangs man on back.)*

MAN *(A little faint.)* I like . . . er I like . . . I'd like to go to the Gents.

WAITER *(Writing on pad.)* 'Jenz'. Ees delicious . . . toop jenz.

MAN No, no I don't want to *eat* the Gents. I want to go to the er 'smallest room'.

WAITER *(Writing.)* 'Small eschtroom' . . . Toop small eschtroom.

GIRL Now you've ordered something called a small eschtroom.

MAN Have I? Lucky I didn't ask for the biggest room.

WAITER Big eschtroom. Toop. English — big stomach — greedy hog huh? Ha ha ha. *(Pats his stomach indicating satiety and does embarrassing burp of politeness.)*

GIRL I'm sorry. I can't stay any longer. This whole place is disgusting.

WAITER Deez gustinks. *(Writes.)* Deez?? *(Indicates it means ten.)* That's a lot of gustinks! *(Shrugs and writes it down, smiling and muttering. Then he turns to man and sees he's not eating, becomes fierce.)* You no eat?????

MAN Oh yes I do . . . often . . . but it all looks so er nice it's a pity to spoil it by eating it . . . er could we er just have the bill?

WAITER Ha! The bill. I fetch. *(Goes out.)*

GIRL I thought you knew all about Goloschnia!

MAN Well . . . I was North of the River Yob. These people are from the South. *(Waiter returns with strange musical instrument.)*

WAITER *(Beaming and indicating instrument.)* Szouzoukia!

MAN This is their local musical instrument. Let him play to us. Er — yes please!

WAITER Schkoiz. *(He empties pepper over their food from the szouzoukia. To girl.)* Kramlock eh? *(Nudges her. Is becoming indecent when the bell sounds. Waiter collects at door a trolley laden with food.)*

MAN   What's all this?

WAITER   *(Going through it dish by dish.)* Toop jenz, toop small eschtroom, toop big eschtroom, und *deez* gustinks! *(This means two frog kebabs, two raw eels in the glass, two tripe-in-the-basket and ten pigs' trotters topped with curry ice cream.)*

MAN   But I asked for the bill!

WAITER   Spayshialitay! *(Whips cloth off dish.)* The bill! *(This is a meringue pie with a toucan's bill sticking out.)*

GIRL   I'm not staying a moment longer.

MAN   They don't understand English. Let's just slip out quietly without paying.

WAITER   *(Drawing huge knife.)* — Without payink is it?

MAN   Or alternatively — *with* paying.

WAITER   Seventeen pound fifty. Thirty pound with V.A.T.

MAN   Thirty pounds? But that's monstrous!

WAITER   Ah! You want a monstrous? *(Brings huge red pumpkin.)* Manager's compliments.

MAN   Oh, all right! *(Gives him three ten pound notes.)* Yes. Thank you very much . . . sorry we didn't er . . . come along let's go . . . There's a little Kanooglik restaurant down the road. It's bound to be better than this . . . *(They go out.)*

WAITER   *(Picking up phone. Dials about three numbers.)* 'Ullo? Kanooglik Caf? Yer, anovver couple of suckers. Yer, thirty nicker. 'Ere Bert, why don't you come over later for a fish and chips, eh?

FACTS ABOUT GOLOSCHNIA.

Since the last sketch was performed many people have written expressing doubts as to the existence of Goloschnia, that relatively unspoiled country in a forgotten corner of the Balkans. We asked the Goloschnian Embassy in Uxbridge to supply us with a tourist map, giving main points of interest. "Get out", they advised. So here is a map of the country drawn from memory. Motorists are advised that they'll need the international green card, some decent wolf-repellent and what else? — a pair of galoshes.

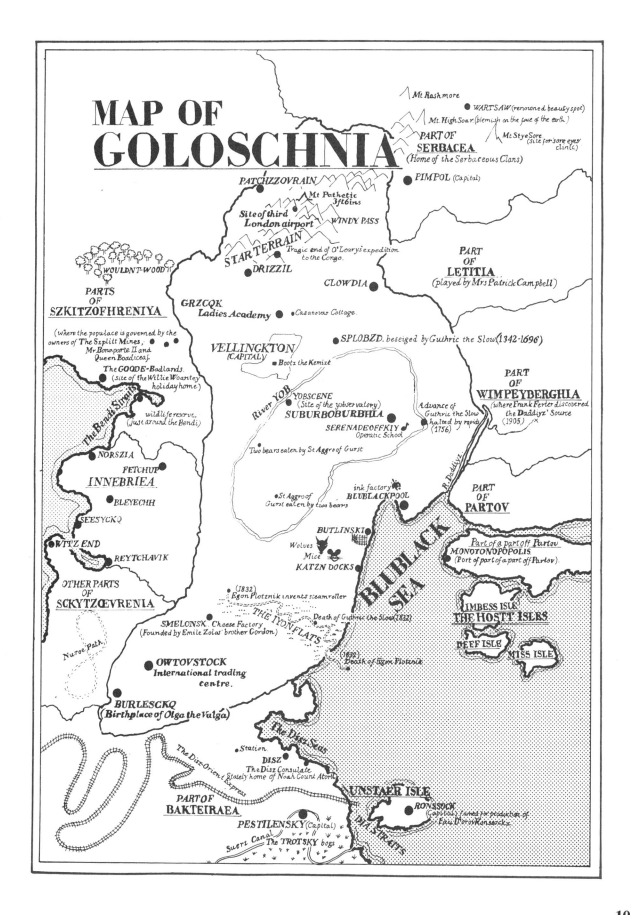

MAP OF GOLOSCHNIA

Mt Rashmore

WARTSAW (renowned beauty spot)

Mt High Soar (blemish on the face of the earth.)

PART OF
SERBACEA
(Home of the Serbaceous Clans)

Mt Stye Sore (Site for sore eyes' clinic.)

PATCHZZOVRAIN

PIMPOL (Capital)

Mt Pathetic
3ft 6ins

Site of third
London airport

WINDY PASS

STAR TERRAIN

Tragic end of O'Leary's expedition
to the Congo.

PART
OF
LETITIA
(played by Mrs Patrick Campbell)

DRIZZIL

WOULDN'T-WOOD

CLOWDIA

PARTS
OF
SZKITZOFHRENIYA

GRZCQK
Ladies Academy

Casanovas Cottage.

(where the populace is governed by the
owners of The Szplitt Mines,
Mr Bonaparte II and
Queen Boadicea).

VELLINGKTON
(CAPITAL)

SPLOBZD. besieged by Guthric the Slow (1342-1696)

Bootz the Kemizt

PART
OF
WIMPEYBERGHIA
(where Frank Ferter discovered
the Daddiyz' Source
(1905.)

The GOODE-Badlands.
(Site of the Willie Woantey
holiday home)

River YOB

YOBSCENE
(Site of the yobservatory)

SUBURBOBURBHIA

Advance of
Guthric the Slow
halted by rapids
(1756)

wildlife reserve.
(Just around the Bendi)

SERENADEOFFKIY
Operatic School

R. Daddiyz

Two bears eaten by St Aggro of Gurst

PART
OF
PARTOV

NORSZIA

FETCHUP
INNEBRIEA

St Aggro of
Gurst eaten by two bears

ink factory
BLUBLACKPOOL

BLEYECHH

Part of a part off Partov
MONOTONOPOPOLIS
(Port of part of a part off Partov)

SEESYCKQ

BUTLINSKI

WITZ END

Wolves
Mice
KATZN DOCKS

**BLUBLACK
SEA**

REYTCHAVIK

OTHER PARTS
OF
SCKYTZŒVRENIA

(1832)
Egon Plotznik invents steamroller

Death of Guthric the Slow (1832)

IMBESS ISLE
THE HOSTT ISLES

Nutroe Path.

THE TYONFLATS

BEEF ISLE

SMELONSK. Cheese Factory
(Founded by Emile Zolas' brother Gordon)

(1832)
Death of Egon Plotznik

MISS ISLE

OWTOVSTOCK
International trading
centre.

BURLESCKQ
(Birthplace of Olga the Vulga)

The Disz-Seas

Station.

The Disz-Orient Express

DISZ
The Disz Consulate
Stately home of Noah Count Atoll

UNSTAER ISLE

RONSSOCK
(Capital) famed for production of
Eau D'otovRonssockz

PART OF
BAKTEIRAEA

PESTILENSKY (Capital)

The TROTSKY bogs

Suerz Canal

DISZTRAITS

SYMBOLS

Ronnie Barker at desk. Small rectangle symbol at bottom right hand corner of picture.

RONNIE BARKER Good evening. As you look at me tonight you will notice two things. One, I'm very handsome, and two, there is a small rectangle at the bottom right hand corner of your picture. This symbol means that the programme you're watching is unsuitable for certain people, so if you're certain people, switch off. For the rest of you, let me explain. What do all our various symbols mean?

105

This rectangle means you shouldn't watch the programme if you're offended by violence.

This symbol means you shouldn't watch if you're offended by rectangles.

This symbol means the programme coming up's going to be a bit naughty.

This symbol means that we haven't given a warning but the programme's going to be naughty just the same so you'll get a nasty shock.

This symbol means absolutely nothing but it was very expensive so we've got to use it. Either that or you're sitting there watching a very old egg.

And this symbol means there's a squashed fly on our camera. But it's not as simple as that.

This symbol tells us a programme will mention the word 'Knickers'.

For those who are offended by the knickers symbol itself, we've got this one:

But what about complaints? I'll just pull the knickers down a bit . . . there. Now this symbol —

Means Mary Whitehouse has phoned, whereas this one —

Means she's beside herself. But we'll also use initials. This —

BB

means the programme will include bare bottoms. This —

CT

means curvaceous thighs, and this —

V

means violence, so if the programme's got the lot you get:

BBC TV

But this —

BBC

only means B.B.C. unless it's the other way up

When it stands for a programme about a bald headed man dreaming of two well developed ladies.

Lastly to save money, we'll use road signs wherever possible: —

means you can only watch the programme if you're over thirty. This sign

means the next programme's gardening club — or possibly David Attenborough in pursuit of the elephant. This one —

would tell you it was going to be the Rolling Stones and you'd get this

for a programme on family planning.

That would be William Tell

And that would be William Don't Tell. While this is quite clearly —

the very last episode of Z cars, and guess what this would be —?

Yes, Father Dear Father.
And when anyone goes on too long you'll get this

Oh. Good night.

THE MANY FACES OF THE TWO RONNIES

So far in the book we've thrilled to the staggering brilliance of the scriptwriters. (Some are brilliant — all are staggering) but let us remember that their words would be a load of dud oysters without the pearls that are the glowing talents of the two stars. A few of the galaxy of faces of the Rons are displayed in these photographs from the pages of Ronnie Corbetts photograph album.

Me with him

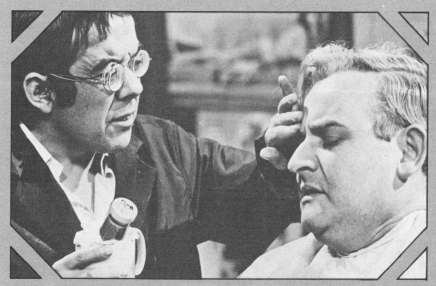

Him with me

Him with small ears
Him with big ears

Us with Josephine Tewson

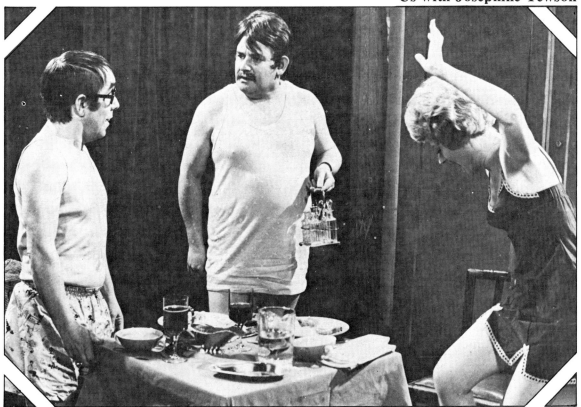

A HUNDRED YEARS ON

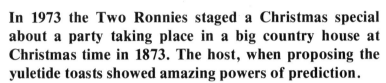

In 1973 the Two Ronnies staged a Christmas special about a party taking place in a big country house at Christmas time in 1873. The host, when proposing the yuletide toasts showed amazing powers of prediction.

THE HOST Well, my friends, we're having a lovely party, though I must say that's the last time I play sardines with young Oscar Wilde.

As I look round at your happy shining faces, I wonder . . . I wonder who's been putting metal polish in the port, but I also wonder what this world will be like in 1973, a hundred years from now.

As Lottie, the chambermaid, was taking off my boots last night, I said, Lottie, you don't have to wear my boots. I'm not that kinky, but she wants to please me. I know how she feels. She feels very nice. But I said, Lottie, you know by 1973, this land of ours will be an earthly paradise! Not only will 'The Mousetrap' still be running but we'll cut the working week to 96 hours. And there'll be equality. Equality for horses, for dogs and even for women. I predict that one of these groups will even want the vote. Yes, there'll be a Horses Liberation Movement, 'Horses Lib' — with their own programme, Horses Favourites. But you know, for years I've been trying to teach Lottie *woman's* rightful position. Suddenly last night I thought of a shining example. I ran into her room and said, 'Grace Darling'. She replied 'For what I am about to receive may the Lord make me truly thankful . . .' What faith!

Oh but 1973 will be wonderful! We'll have a thirty horsepower bus worked by only two men, one to drive and the other to clean up after the thirty horses. Yes, and there'll be flying machines. Here is my design for an aircraft with two engines.

Look at the inventions we're already making! We have the sandwich invented by the Earl of Sandwich. What great things we expect from Lord Wimpey and the Duke of Jumbo Brunchburger! And look at this kettle — this is the very kettle that James Watt saw when he first thought of the steam engine. Had he come in five minutes later the tea would have been made, the frying pan would have been on the stove and Watt would have invented the chip engine.

My own field, as you know, is animal husbandry. Leave the room, Mellors! In a hundred years we'll breed fair-isle sheep like this, already knitted.

And at this very moment I'm working on a two-faced cow. No, I don't mean Lottie. Look at the advantages!

It can't run away, you get double cream — and it's house trained.

Now, you three gardeners at the back there. Listen well. In 1973 your great grandsons could be men of power, yes, you, Zebediah Heath, old Diggory Wilson and you, Sambo Powell.

Ladies and Gentlemen, I give you, the future!

REACTIONS.
If a comedy director doesn't always point the cameras at the person who's speaking, it's because the reactions of the listener can be more interesting. This next sketch which featured a girl talking over the address system in a hotel, was full of reactions from the Ronnies. Reactions — in this case — to the agonizing problem of

EMBARRASSING NAMES

A rather top class hotel lounge. Seven men sitting around. One is an army major in uniform, one is an archdeacon in clerical garb, one is a normal looking young man, one is a rather twittish looking young man, one is a distinguished looking older man. One of the Ronnies is a northern alderman, proudly wearing a chain of office. The other is an obvious old Etonian type. The Tannoy bursts into life.

TANNOY (GIRL)   There is a message for Admiral Sir Compost Heap. Will Admiral Sir Compost Heap please come to reception.

(They all look at each other with the possibility in their minds that Admiral Sir Compost Heap might be among them. Nobody moves or speaks.)

TANNOY   Message for Admiral Sir Compost Heap. Will Admiral Sir Compost Heap please come to reception.

OLDER MAN   *(Looking at watch.)* Oh . . . practically five bells. Think I'll take a turn round the Prom before dinner. *(He goes out.)*

NORTHERNER   *(To the room.)* Round the Prom! Pull the other one, it's got five bells on it. He were Admiral Sir Compost Heap.

ETONIAN   No doubt about it. Fellow was scared we'd be laughing at him because of his name.

NORTHERNER   As if we'd laugh at someone just because of his name. It wasn't his fault he were called Compost Heap. It were his parents fault for being called Compost Heap in first place. No call to laugh at that . . . *(Pause, laughing.)* Aye though . . . Compost bloody Heap!

ETONIAN   I used to take out a girl once called Angela Compost Heap. I think she was one of the Somerset Compost Heaps.

NORTHERNER   Aye. There's a load of compost heaps down that way. *(Pause.)*

TANNOY We have a telegram for Mr. Algernon Bedpan. Will Mr. Algernon Bedpan please come to reception. *(They all look round again.)*

TWITTISH MAN *(Getting up embarrassedly.)* Er . . . just nipping off to the Gents . . . *(Exit.)*

NORTHERNER Well he's not going to Gents for a kick off. *He's* Algernon Bedpan. It stands out a mile.

ETONIAN Yes well, hardly need to go the Gents really, if his name's Bedpan . . . Ha ha! Sorry.

ARCHDEACON Seems uncharitable to laugh at people because of their names . . . but really — Bedpan! It does have its light side. Ha ha ha!

TANNOY There's a young lady at reception asking for Archdeacon Randy . . . Archdeacon Randy please. *(The others look at the Archdeacon.)*

ARCHDEACON Oh well . . . sitting here won't get the sermon written will it? *(Exit.)*

NORTHERNER Randy by name, randy by nature eh?

ETONIAN I knew a girl called Virginia Randy once. Embarrassing thing. She married a man called Henry Drawers. Now she's . . .

NORTHERNER Don't tell me . . . don't tell me. I can see it coming.

ETONIAN Lady Fosgrove.

NORTHERNER Oh.

TANNOY We have an emergency call for Major Disaster. Major Disaster please. *(The others look round and then they look at the major sitting there in his uniform.)*

MAJOR All right. *I'm* Major Disaster. I'm not ashamed of it. What's in a name? *(Gets up and falls over a chair.)* Blast! *(Exits clumsily.)*

NORTHERNER Disaster by name, disaster by nature I always say.

ETONIAN Damned good military name. There've been Disasters at every British battle since Agincourt.

TANNOY Will Mr. Cornelius Van der Pouf please come to the Manager's office. Mr. Cornelius Van der Pouf.

ORDINARY LOOKING MAN Ha! I vunder who zis vos for? Who iss zis Van der Pouf? Vell . . . I off for der noggin now go. Cheery by mein fellow Englishmenz. *(He minces off.)*

NORTHERNER He were a Dutchman or I'm a pouf.

ETONIAN Must be awful having an embarrassing name.

NORTHERNER Aye. *(Pause. They look at each other.)*

ETONIAN Er . . . I don't think I quite caught *your* name . . . ?

NORTHERNER No. I don't suppose you did. *(Pause.)*

TANNOY Will Mr. Ivor Bignose please go to the kiosk where a message awaits him. Calling Mr. Ivor Bignose.

BOTH Ivor Bignose! So that's your name! No no no! *I'm* not Ivor Bignose. Oh. *(They laugh.)*

(A man with an enormous nose walks through.)

NORTHERNER Bignose by name —

ETONIAN Bignose by nature. Ha ha. I'm er sorry. I thought for one moment that you were called Bignose.

NORTHERNER That's all right lad. No skin off my er nose as it were. I'm not daft. If my name *were* Bignose I wouldn't come to a place with one of these bloody loudspeakers.

ETONIAN Golly no!

TANNOY We have a message for Alderman Fatpimple. Will Alderman Fatpimple please go to the foyer and meet Mrs. Fatpimple.

ETONIAN *Fat*pimple??

NORTHERNER Well, er I'd er best be off then.

ETONIAN Yes. Nice to have met you, Mr. Fatpimple. We don't want to keep Mrs. Fatpimple waiting, do we? Nor all the little fatty watty pimples, eh?

NORTHERNER I can't help my name. *(Trudges off towards the exit, utterly defeated. A waiter enters and drops his tray.)*

WAITER Oh Knickers!!

ETONIAN Yes? Who called me?

(Fatpimple collapses with laughter and points at Mr O'Knickers who registers extreme misery.)

HELLO

Party Music
Ronnie Barker standing with drink. Ronnie Corbett comes up to him.

RC Hello.

        RB I'm sorry?

RC I just said "Hello".

        RB Sorry? Sorry? I didn't catch it again.

RC Hello.

        RB What?

RC Hello!

        RB And . . .

RC And what?

        RB And what else did you say besides "hello"?

RC I didn't say anything else. I just said "hello".

        RB Not — "Hello, you boring old git, who the hell invited you?"

RC No I didn't say that.

        RB Oh! I don't mean those exact words . . . I was only using them as an example . . . It might have been more on the lines of: "Hello, you fat, ugly, mealy-mouthed sadist, I wish you were dead . . ."

RC No . . . I didn't say anything apart from "Hello".

        RB Huh! I've only got your word for it.

RC Look . . . I was over the other side of the room, I saw nobody was talking to you, and I thought I'd just come over and say "Hello".

        RB I never did!

RC What?

        RB You implied that Dorothy and I were having a relationship.

RC When?

        RB Just then! All that stuff about my car not being in the garage.

RC I didn't say anything about your car . . .

        RB Oh no . . . but you *implied* it!

RC All I said was "Hello".

        RB Oh yes, but look at the way you said it!

RC What?

        RB You said it in that "Hello! His-car-wasn't-in-the-garage-at-11.30-and-he-left-the-light-on-in-the-study-to-make-the-wife-think-he-was-working-late" — kind of way.

RC It wasn't meant to sound like that. It was just a "Hello, how-are-you?"

        RB Oh I see! "Hello-how-*are*-you . . . going-to-explain-the-hotpants-in-the-glove-compartment-when-the-wife-gives-the-vicar-a-lift-on-Sunday?"

RC It was only "Hello".

RB Listen, sonny, if you go round talking to everybody the way you've been talking to me, I'm not surprised you haven't any friends.

RC I've got lots of friends.

RB Oh yes . . . but they all ran out on you and you had to come over and pick on me to heap abuse on!

RC I only said "Hello".

RB I mean, how was *I* to know it was loaded?

RC What?

RB The gun! The gun you said . . .

RC I said "Hello".

RB Anyway I was going to throw it away and never use it . . . it was Dorothy who wanted to have a look down the barrel and see how fast the bullets came out.

RC I just said "Hello".

RB I tried to stop her . . . But before I could, she'd pulled the trigger, jumped out of the car and buried herself under a bush on a lonely stretch of the A47 outside Stafford.

RC I was only using the word "Hello" to start a little convers . . .

RB And now I come to think of it, I was in Glasgow at the time in any case — no, Frankfurt! . . . No! Even further away . . . er . . . Istanbul: I was in a cellar — chained — all by myself . . . *(Pause)* except for the *witnesses* . . . lots of witnesses . . . Turks . . . but they *write* in English . . . *They'd* testify . . . you could write to them . . . unless they're dead . . . oh come to think of it, I think they are dead! Yes I think I read about them being dead . . . pity . . . You've got to believe me! You've got to!

RC *(Embarrassed)* I only came up to him and said "Hello".

RB In any case I didn't mean to . . . but she kept on about the money and the divorce and the gambling and the bad breath . . . I just *had* to! *(His voice rising to a crescendo)* All right I've been a fool! A bloody fool! I admit it!

RC A perfectly ordinary "Hello" . . .

RB *(A manic glint in his eye)* But you'll never take me alive! *Whips out a phial, tears off the top with his teeth and slips it in his martini and swigs it down, dying with many contortions and assorted terrible death convulsions.*
At last he lies dead at Ronnie C's feet. RC looks over him anxiously . . .

RC Hello? . . . *(Cautiously)* Hello? Hellooo? *(No reaction . . .*
RC stands up) Tut tut . . . Can't have a decent conversation with anyone nowadays . . .

Pull out fast to reveal RC standing alone amidst a roomful of dead guests. All have glasses, some are draped over tables, most are on the floor.

RC starts to pick his way through them, picking up the odd head with his foot, saying "hello" hopefully and letting it drop again. Fade.

We're sorry about all the sex and violence in this book but we were told that's what people like at the festive season. Well, it makes a change from good will. Anyway, those who mention sex and violence usually talk about Michael Palin and Terry Jones in the very next breath — especially if they're breathing out. Mike and Terry are two fifths of Monty Python and of course, had very disturbed childhoods.

When you're like this you either go in for psychotherapy or write great sketches for television. They went in for psychotherapy . . .

SLAP UP PARTY

A party. Ronnie B. Stands in a dinner jacket sipping wine. Ronnie C. approaches.

RC Hello.
(RB slaps him. RC smiles and looks round uncertainly. There is a pause.)

RC Jolly good party.
(RB Slaps him again. RC looks round even more embarrassed. He tries again cautiously.)

RC The . . . er . . . the wine's not . . . bad . . . is it?
(He waits for a moment. RB does not slap him. RC loosens up.)

RC My name's . . . *(RB slaps him twice.)* . . . look! What is this?

RB I'm terribly sorry . . . it's just something I can't control. If I were you, I'd move away.

RC Well . . .
(RB slaps him.)

RB Everyone does. I'm used to it. I won't be offended.

RC *(Understandingly)* Well it seems a shame . . . *(RB slaps him)* . . . just to *walk off* . . . er . . . perhaps if I *duck* when I see your hand coming across . . . we could have . . . er . . . quite a reasonable conversation . . .
(RB makes to slap him . . . he ducks. The slap misses.)

RC There we are!
(RB kicks him on the shin.)

RC *(Indignantly)* Ow!

RB I'm terribly sorry. I should have warned you about that. I really am sorry.

RC *(Nursing leg)* Ooh! That jolly well hurt!

RB *(Sincerely)* I know! *(Desperately)* I know! It's awful! I haven't any friends left . . . Oh! I tell people my trouble. They try to be kind . . . they try to help me and then . . . I kick them . . . *(Starts to sob)* I can't go on. I'm at my wits end.

RC *(Making a big effort)* I'm sorry . . . I didn't mean to lose
my temper.
(RB slaps him again.)

> **RB** *(Nobly)* No . . . You go off . . . enjoy yourself . . . I'll
> manage . . . There's nothing *you* can do . . . there's nothing
> *anyone* can do . . .

RC There must be something. *(RC skilfully avoids a slap
and a kick)* Have you thought of seeing a psychiatrist?
*(RB gets a salmon from inside his coat and hits RC over the
head with it.)*

> **RB** Psychiatrist! What do I need a psychiatrist for? *(RB
> reaches in his coat and gets out a bag of flour.)* He'll only say
> I'm mad . . .
> *(RB empties packet of flour over RC. There is a pregnant
> pause, during which RC marshalls all his powers of
> understanding and speaks earnestly.)*

RC *(Earnestly)* But you're *not* mad . . . are you?

> **RB** Good lord no! *(RB produces an icing gun with a plunger
> and procedes to ice RC's head, talking as he does so.)* But
> this is the trouble . . . I *want* to be liked . . . I *need* to be
> liked, but I just can't help it . . .
> *(He sticks a wafer on RC's head on top of the icing and slaps
> him. There is another pause.)*

RC *(Long sufferingly wiping face and wiping icing from
hair)* Look . . . I don't want to hurt your feelings . . . but I
feel that . . . perhaps I ought to go . . . I'm sorry . . . God!
It's so pathetic of me! To be unable to come to terms with
this problem of yours . . . But . . . forgive me . . . I'm
sorry . . .

> **RB** Well thanks for trying. *(RB picks up a lemon meringue
> pie from a trolley beside him and pushes it in RC's face.)*

RC *(Giving RB a manly pat on the shoulder)* Well anyway
. . . no hard feeling, old chap . . .
*(RC turns. As he walks away RB kicks him. Another party
guest turns to RB.)*

OTHER PARTY GUEST Hello Ronnie!

> **RB** *(Enthusiastically)* Hello, Charles! *(Nodding towards RC)*
> Oh dear, I thought I'd never get rid of him.

We end this book with a party — for only two people. Over seven series of TV shows the Ronnies have proved that two people can be quite a party . . . Oh, I'm a smooth-talking so and so! But seriously, the lights dim, the shadows lengthen; bring on the clowns, bring on the clichés, bring on the last sketch . . . let's get *on* with it then. Right.

THE TWO MAN PARTY

(A party scene. There are no guests, but there are large numbers of glasses and a liberal display of canapés and snacks. The host is dusting the canapés with a feather duster. The bell rings. He puts the feather duster away. The bell rings again.)

HOST All right, all right, no need to wear out the bell push. Bloody great thumbs all over it. *(Opens door. Guest enters.)* Hullo, hullo, come in. Step over the mat, would you, it's a new one.

(The guest steps over the mat.)

GUEST Hullo. Hope I'm not too late. *(Sees that there is nobody else there.)* Oh, am I early?

HOST No, we're in full swing. Come and join the fun.

GUEST Oh, thank you. Not very many people seem to have come.

HOST Oh, I don't know. It's a better turn out than last year. Not like in the old days, though. Sometimes we used to get as many as two or three all in one evening.

GUEST Oh, an orgy.

HOST Now, have a drink. What'll you have? There's water or if you like something a bit stronger there's melted ice.

GUEST Oh well in that case . . . er . . . I think I'll plump for water.

HOST Right. Say when. *(Pours water.)*

GUEST When. *(Host stops pouring.)*

HOST Anything with it?

GUEST Well have you anything to dilute it with . . . whisky, brandy, gin, to make it go further?

HOST No, I haven't. I thought you were going to bring a bottle. It *is* a bottle party.

GUEST Oh, I'm sorry. Well in that case I'll just have a dash of water with it.

(Host gives him a dash of water.)

HOST Cheers.

GUEST Cheers. *(They drink.)*

HOST That'll put hairs on your chest. *(Guest sits down.)* Look, I'm sorry, but I've forgotten your name. Awfully difficult to remember everyone's name at a party.

GUEST It's Wilfred.

HOST Of course. Look, Wilfred, one small thing, if you don't mind terribly. You are rather wearing out that chair.

GUEST Oh I'm frightfully sorry. How thoughtless of me. *(Stands.)* Anyway, I prefer standing. I can't stand sitting down. I say, that's good, isn't it? I can't stand sitting down. Ha ha ha ha ha. Ha ha ha ha ha ha.

HOST Please don't laugh too much. It may seem a niggling point, but it uses up all the air.

GUEST Oh sorry, I must leave some for everyone else. After all, guests abhor a vacuum. Ha ha ha . . . sorry.

HOST That's all right, Wilfred. Come and have some solid refreshment.

GUEST Oh good, I haven't eaten all day. Mmmm, these look delicious. *(Takes a canapé, bites, cries out.)*

          HOST Nice?

GUEST Yes, it's . . . er . . . delicious . . . but it's made of wood, isn't it?

          HOST That's right. I use the same one every year.

GUEST There's only one thing. I . . . er . . . bit of a fad, I suppose, but I don't eat wood a lot.

          HOST Well they aren't all wooden. It'd be a funny party where all the food was wooden. There's one vol au vent that's real, but I've hidden it.

GUEST Oh what fun. We'll play spot the vol au vent . . . and after that I can hide in a cupboard and play sardine.

          HOST Oh, go easy on the cheese straws, would you? They don't grow on trees.

GUEST *(Wincing as he bites a wooden cheese straw.)* Ouch! I er rather think this one did.

          HOST Oh, I think the party's going to be a success. Have another water.

GUEST No thanks, I'm driving.

          HOST Go on, be a devil. Live a little.

GUEST Well just a tiny one then. *(Host pours it.)*

          HOST One tiny niggle, Wilfred. You are rather wearing out the carpet. Would you mind awfully standing on one leg?

GUEST Not at all. Which leg would you like me to stand on?

          HOST Either leg, my dear fellow. This is a party. It's Liberty Hall.

          (Guest begins to hop.)

GUEST I don't want to seem churlish, but aren't you using all *your* legs?

          HOST Good point. You've got me there. I haven't got a leg to stand on. *(Also starts to hop.)*

GUEST *(Pointing at empty frame on wall.)* I like your empty frame.

HOST It's an original. Here, have one of these. *(Hands guest a paper hat, puts one on himself. They continue to hop.)*

GUEST Ah. 'Merry Christmas, 1938' I say, things are really warming up now!

HOST Good party, isn't it?

GUEST Much better than the local hop. Ha ha ha ha . . . sorry.

HOST Have one of these, go on. *(Hands him one of those things you blow out that writers never know the name of.)*

GUEST Thank you. *(They both work the blowers.)* I say, the frost's beginning to melt on your radiators.

HOST It never did that at all last year. It's you, making things go with a swing.

GUEST It's very kind of you to say so.

HOST It's true. You're the life and soul of the party.

GUEST Thank you.

HOST By the way, can I have my invitation back? I can use it again next year.

GUEST *(Ceasing to hop.)* Actually I haven't got one. I'm a gate crasher.

HOST What? Get out, you filthy little worm. Abusing my hospitality. Get out. *(Pushes guest towards door.)* And mind the mat. *(Guest steps over mat.)*

GUEST I'm sorry, I only wanted a bit of fun.

HOST Get out . . . and try not to tread on too many of the stairs.

(Guest exits. Enormous crash off. Host calls out.)

HOST Thank you. *(Picks up guest's glass.)* What a world we live in. He thinks he can barge in here any year just because he's my brother.

(He carefully measures unused water back into the jug.)

Well, there you are. Some bits and pieces written on buses and trains, in offices and teashops and most of all, in pubs up and down the country. If you've enjoyed reading them as much as we did writing them, it means you've had enough! So don't drive!